My Egyptian Grandmother's Kitchen

Magda
Mehdawy

My Egyptian Grandmother's Kitchen

Traditional Dishes
Sweet and
Savory

The American University in Cairo Press
Cairo   New York

To my three daughters:
I dedicate this book to you
so that it may be an aid
in the preparation
of all the foods I made
that you loved so much

The American University in Cairo Press
113 Sharia Kasr el Aini, Cairo, Egypt
420 Fifth Avenue, New York, NY 10018
www.aucpress.com

First published in Arabic as *Matbakh giddati* in 2004
Translated by Dr. Mariam S. Tanagho

Dar el Kutub No. 2827/05
ISBN 978 977 424 927 3

5 6 7 8   24 23 22 21 20

Printed in Egypt

Contents

Introduction

People in Egypt have grown accustomed to eating the ready-made meals now commonly available in the market that have come to us from different countries.

They are even preparing them at home themselves, using them to replace our traditional healthy meals, in spite of their high content of fats, carbohydrates, and artificial ingredients (such as colors, flavors, and scents). These foods are usually cooked in oils that have been boiled for extended periods, which are harmful in the long run.

With the progression of scientific discovery in the field of nutrition, the value of our old-fashioned foods has become evident. Even the sweets and snacks children love such as *'asaliya* (a molasses candy), *simsimiya* (a sesame candy), nougat, toffee, and biscuits, as well as *dum* (the fruit of the doum palm), *kharub* (carob), *libb* (watermelon and pumpkin seeds), peanuts, chickpeas, and sugarcane have been found to have good nutritional benefits.

If we carefully watch what we eat, returning to our native foods and preparing them at home ourselves, we will be able to avoid unhealthy, artificial ingredients, and ensure quality, cleanliness, and economy.

In cooking Egyptian meals, we can eliminate or reduce the excessive use of fats and ghee, and replace them with vegetable oils such as olive, corn, and linseed oil.

This book was a personal experience for me as I grew up watching my grand-mother cooking most of these dishes and I enjoy preparing them for my small family. I pray to God that I have been successful in what I set out to do and that the final outcome is of value to anyone seeking traditional Egyptian food.

Magda Mehdawy

About the Egyptian Kitchen in the Pharaonic Era

The Egyptian kitchen as it is today is considered a legacy from our ancestors, the pharaohs. The vegetables, grains, and legumes used today in Egypt are very much like the ones our forefathers cultivated and harvested for food. In fact, Egyptian farmers today still depend on the Coptic calendar, which is based on the pharaonic calendar, for planting and harvesting their crops.

We have been able to learn a lot about the daily life and agricultural habits of the early Egyptians from their recordings on papyrus. We know today that they planted green mallow, lettuce, green chickpeas, chicory, cabbage, green onions, garlic, artichokes, and olives. We also know that they grew broad beans, lentils, rice, barley, wheat, lupines, fenugreek, aniseed, sesame, dates, grapes, black cumin, and liquorice and sycamore.

We also know that the ancient Egyptians raised cattle and sheep, and hunted deer. They raised ducks, geese, and pigeons and knew how to catch fish and preserve by salting. They knew how to extract salt from seawater. They kept bees for honey and pressed oil from sesame seeds for cooking. They also used colocynth (a very bitter plant, like cactus) and castor oil, used for cosmetics. Oils unfit for consumption (such as linseed) were used as lamp oil, as bases for paints to decorate the walls of tombs, temples, and shrines, and in the making of perfumes and cosmetics.

The ancient Egyptians gave special importance to the kitchen. The room farthest away from the entrance of the house was always used as the kitchen, with a roof made from branches and hay to shield the interior from the sun while still allowing ventilation. In one corner of the kitchen was the clay-covered oven for baking, with several shelves inside for placing earthenware containers at different levels. On the kitchen floor was a large mortar and pestle for grinding grains.

A large mixing bowl for making dough was always found adjacent to a kitchen wall; since it was made of clay it was lime coated. Some of the houses had a storage room above the kitchen, similar to today's cellars. Until the beginning of the twentieth century, Egyptian houses still had these cellars.

Ancient Egyptians also brewed beer from barley. Earthenware pots containing evidence of beer have been found in tombs, and tomb paintings depicting the essentials of the afterlife include bread and beer, which was called *henket*.

Beer was prepared by soaking either barley bread or toasted barley grains in water for 24 hours, and then drying the mixture in the sun and open air.

It would then be soaked in water for five more hours, strained, and put in a warm place to ferment. Lupine was used to flavor the beer, giving it a slightly bitter taste. The Egyptians also prepared *buzza*, a type of beer today called 'pharaonic wine' in Upper Egypt, by wetting fresh, green wheat grains and placing them in a clay pot for 24 hours to sprout. A yeast dough was made and flavored with anise and fennel seeds, then fermented and served. After sugar came to Egypt it could be used to sweeten *buzza*. This same technique is still being used today in Upper Egypt, where people prepare this drink on special occasions linked to pharaonic feasts which have continued as part of the culture through the Coptic Christian religion. The celebration of *Shamm al-Nisim* in the spring is one example of a festival when foods we traditionally eat reflect the pharaonic influence on various aspects of our daily lives.

Scales in Ancient Egypt

Egypt had measures and scales of its own that were in use since ancient times and up until the middle of the twentieth century. These were:

Drachma = (about 3.25 grams)
Ounce = 12 drachma (about 40 grams)
Pound = 144 drachma (about 450 grams)
Oke = 400 drachma (about 1250 grams)

Special measures for grains were also used, such as:

Wheat measure = 10 okes
Cup = 1/2 wheat measure = 5 okes wheat
Quarter *(Ruba')* = 1/4 wheat measure = 2 1/2 okes wheat

Measures differed in weight according to the different types of grains being measured; for example, a certain volume of wheat differed in weight from the same volume of lentils, and so forth.

Starting in the late 1950s, Egypt began using the metric system.
1 kilogram = 1000 grams
1/2 kilogram = 500 grams
1/4 kilogram = 250 grams

Scales and Measures Used in this Book

T his book uses weight in kilograms as its unit of measurement. In some cases, measurements were done using a standardized cup or spoon.

To accurately measure dry ingredients, heap them in the cup or spoon and level off at the rim with a knife drawn across the top. Liquids are measured in liters.

Volume and Weight Equivalents

Dry Measures

1 teaspoon = 5 grams

1 tablespoon = 15 grams

1 large cup flour = 120 grams

8 large cups flour = 1 kilogram

1 large cup rice = 225 grams

4 large cups rice = 1 kilogram

1 large cup butter = 200 grams

5 large cups butter = 1 kilogram

1 large cup sugar = 200 grams

5 large cups sugar = 1 kilogram

Wet Measures

1 large cup ghee or oil = 225 grams

4 large cups water = 1 liter

4 large cups oil = 1 liter

Oven Temperatures

Description	$^{\circ}$C	Oven Control Key
Low oven	120°	C1
Warm oven	150°	C2
Medium low heat	$160^{\circ}-179^{\circ}$	C3
Medium heat	$180^{\circ}-199^{\circ}$	C4
Medium high heat	$200^{\circ}-219^{\circ}$	C5
Hot oven	$220^{\circ}-239^{\circ}$	C6
Very hot oven	$240^{\circ}-259^{\circ}$	C7

Calories

A calorie is the amount of energy required to raise the temperature of one gram of water by one degree Celsius.

A kilocalorie (kcal) is the amount of energy required to raise the temperature of 1000 grams of water by one degree Celsius. It equals 1000 calories. The kilocalorie is the unit by which we measure the heat and energy given by foods.

Foods differ in their caloric contents according to their composition. For example, 1 gram of carbohydrate furnishes 4 calories of energy to the body. Fats and proteins supply 9 and 4 calories per gram respectively.

The only components of foods we eat that are metabolized by the body to generate heat and energy are carbohydrates, proteins, and fats. Individuals require different amounts of calories each day. Following are some representative daily calorific guidelines:

Children aged 4–6 years—1700 calories.

Children aged 7–12 years—2500 calories.

Adolescents aged 13–15 years — 3500 calories.

Female adolescents aged 16–18 years—2400 calories.

Male adolescents aged 16–18 years—2600 calories.

Adult males—2800 calories.

Adult females—2200 calories.

Pregnant females—2800 calories.

The following are examples of the caloric contents of some of the foods frequently used in this book.

1 cup flour (120g) = 444 calories

1 cup rice (225g) = 825 calories

1 cup butter (200g) = 1506 calories

1 cup ghee or oil (225g) = 1687 calories

1 cup sugar (200g) = 800 calories

1 teaspoon sugar (5g) = 20 calories

1 tablespoon sugar (15g) = 60 calories

The Storage Cupboard

B asic ingredients should always be available in the cupboard to facilitate the preparation of various foods. They can be bought every month, and put in glass jars or well-sealed containers for easy access and storage. Label the containers, and put all similar items together on the same shelf.

Store only what you are likely to use in a month's time to avoid spoilage. If you are buying new stock, make sure to first use up the leftovers before opening the fresh ingredients.

Components of the Storage Cupboard

Grains and Legumes

• **Rice** The well-known Egyptian rice (arborio rice) is frequently used in the Egyptian kitchen to prepare all types of rice dishes, stuffings and even desserts. It is good rice with a distinctive flavor. Equal proportions of rice and water are used in cooking it, and no additional liquid is needed during cooking.

If storing rice for longer than 6 months, add one quarter cup of coarse salt for every five kilograms rice to protect it from infestation by mites and worms.

• **Yellow lentils** are used in a variety of dishes from soups to main courses.

• **Brown lentils** are yellow lentils but whole, with the shell. High in nutritional value, they are used stewed or with rice and macaroni (*migaddara*) or as a salad.

• **Broad beans** can be stored whole or crushed and are used in the preparation of several main dishes. They can be stewed at home in a special pot for that purpose. They can also be soaked for 24 hours, then placed in a colander and covered with a wet cloth to sprout, and used in many delicious and healthy recipes that can be eaten on a regular basis.

• **White beans (great northern beans)** are stewed with or without meat eaten as not in salad.

• **Blackeyed peas** are used in the same way as white beans but have a different flavor.

- **Cracked wheat** is whole wheat grain that has been cracked, boiled and sun-dried. It is used in many foods.
- **Wholewheat grains** are the whole, uncrushed wheat grains that are used in making *bilila* and *'ashura*.
- **Local (small) chickpeas** are green chickpeas that have been shelled and dried. They are a component of many dishes and must be soaked for around 1 hour before use.
  - **Chickpeas (garbanzo beans)** are another type of dried, whole chickpeas that are larger in size. They also are a component of many dishes and require 8 hours of soaking, then boiling, before use. Therefore, if planning to use them in a recipe, begin to soak them the previous evening.
  - **Wheat flour** is essential for the preparation of all types of dishes.
  - **Wheat bran** is the outer layer of the wheat grain that is separated in the process of making white flour. It is highly nutritious, containing large amounts of vitamin B complex. It is used in making bread and for coating fish for grilling.
- **Cornmeal** comes from grinding white corn. It is used to make bread, and cornmeal cakes.

- **Pasta (macaroni)** comes in many different shapes. Store only small amounts to avoid spoilage. Have available the different forms of pasta such as spaghetti, vermicelli, rosa marina, tiny rice-shaped pasta pieces for soups, and penne or manicotti for béchamel.
- **Semolina flour** is used for making different types of desserts such as *basbusa, harisa* and, *ma'mula* filling.

Vegetables

- **Onions** are an essential part of most dishes. Look for old onions with red skins, as they are drier and keep longer without spoiling. Store onions tied up in large bunches and hang in a well-ventilated sunny place, such as a balcony.
- **Garlic** is also an ingredient in many dishes. Look for dry bulbs with large cloves for easier peeling. To facilitate peeling, soak cloves in cold water for 5 minutes. Store garlic tied up in large bunches and hang like onions.
- **Potatoes** are tuberous vegetables that easily spoil, turn soft and sprout after a while if kept at room temperature. They should be stored in a cool, dry, and dark place. They can be served in a variety of ways, frequently fried as side dishes.
- **Cooking oils** It is better to buy natural ghee and to avoid shortening (synthetic

9

ghee), as it is high in cholesterol and saturated fats, which can cause heart disease.

- **Corn or sunflower oil** can be used directly on salads or in combination with ghee in preparing cooked foods.
- **Cottonseed oil** is used for deep frying.
- **Olive oil** is used for salads and for cooking.
- **Linseed oil** is very healthy, but spoils easily. It must be used immediately and is best not stored for lengthy periods of time. Linseed oil should be stored in the refrigerator.
- **White vinegar** is made from sugarcane in a 5% concentration. It is used in salad dressings and in the preparation of different foods, particularly seafood.

Essential Ingredients for Preparing Beverages and Desserts

- **White sugar**
- **Black tea** comes in the form of teabags, which are placed in hot water, or in the form of a fine powder or granules, which are used for the preparation of boiled tea and tea infusions, called *kushari* tea in Egypt.
- **Green tea** comes in a roughly ground form to be boiled or infused. It is best taken after heavy meals as it aids digestion. It is beneficial for the stomach and

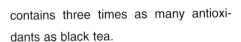
contains three times as many antioxidants as black tea.

- **Dried mint** is used as an infusion, and in the preparation of several dishes, particularly salads.
- **Powdered milk** is dried, full-cream milk. Water is added in a ratio of 3:1, yielding reconstituted, sterilized and pasteurized milk.
- **Sesame seeds**, white and red.
- **Black cumin**
- **Baking soda** can be purchased from any spice dealer and is used as a raising agent.
- **Dry yeast** can be found in supermarkets and is used as a raising agent.
- **Baking powder** can be found in supermarkets and is used in desserts as a raising agent.
- **Vanilla** is also in most supermarkets in Egypt and is used to add a pleasant smell to desserts containing eggs. It is more commonly sold in powdered form.
- **Nuts** (walnuts, almonds, hazelnuts) must be stored in a refrigerator or a freezer as they spoil easily if exposed to high temperatures.
- **Raisins, dried prunes, dried apricots, grated coconut, pressed pitted dates**

- **Sugar syrup** for use in oriental desserts
- **Molasses**, called *'asal aswad* (black honey), is made in Upper Egypt where *qasab* (sugar cane) is planted. It can be found in supermarkets.
- **Cornstarch** is the flour ground from the heart of the corn kernel. It is used as a thickening agent in sauces. Also known as cornflour, it is available in most supermarkets and grocers.
- **Tahini** is a thick paste made from ground sesame seeds.

Ingredients that Must be Kept Refrigerated

These are foods that spoil at room temperature (25°C) and must therefore be stored in the refrigerator (4°C) :

Cheese, eggs, fresh vegetables, fruits, fresh milk, cream, heavy cream, yogurt and broth that is used as a soup base.

Foods that spoil easily such as meats and poultry must be stored in a freezer at a temperature of 20°C. Fish is better bought and used fresh. If fish must be stored in the freezer, do not keep it for more than one week to retain its freshness and nutritional value.

Spices, Dried Herbs, and Condiments

The Egyptian kitchen includes a large number of spices that are frequently used in recipes in different combinations. Spices are added to appetizers to give distinctive flavors and aromas, and to aid digestion. Due to their many medicinal benefits, spices are also considered a pharmacy within hand's reach, giving those who use them health and strength.

We will mention the health benefits of each spice to allow the reader to make safe choices for rapid healing with no side effects.

Spices and condiments are best bought in their unground forms. They should be toasted and ground just before use, or in very small quantities, and stored in tightly sealed jars. This retains their characteristic flavors and odors.

- **Aniseed *(Yansun)*** These are dry seeds with a hot, bitter taste. They have a pungent flavor and aroma and are used in many desserts and biscuits. Aniseeds are considered to have antispasmodic, antitussive, and appetite stimulant properties.
- **Bay Leaf *(Waraq Lawra)*** These are large, smooth, bright tree leaves with a pleasant odor and a bitter taste. They are used in soup and in combination with other spices. Bay leaves are believed to

improve gastric and chest conditions and act as an antiflatulent.

• **Caraway *(Carawia)*** These seeds have an oblong, beadlike shape and a pleasing taste. They are used in many dishes, both savory and sweet. They are commonly used in *kahk*, the traditional biscuits baked for feasts. Caraway seeds are used as an antiflatulent and gastrointestinal stimulant. They also help fight colds, stimulate milk production in lactating mothers, and relieve uterine pains following childbirth.

• **Cardamom *(Habbahan)*** Known to the ancient Egyptians by the name of *hal* from which came its Arabic name, these are large, green seed pods containing small, black granules. The seeds are added to different foods to improve flavor and are ground with coffee beans to make Arabic coffee. They are considered to be an antiflatulent and stimulant, and to aid digestion.

• **Cinnamon *(Qirfa)*** Cinnamon is available as a powder or as sticks. It is used in the seasoning of many foods, particularly biscuits and desserts due to its highly aromatic smell. Cinnamon soothes indigestion, stimulates the intestines, and is an antiflatulent and an appetite stimulant.

• **Cloves *(Qurunful)*** These are black, flower-like buds with stems that resemble small nails. They contain aromatic oils which give them their distinctive, penetrating smell, and they have multiple medicinal benefits. They are used in seasoning meats and also in desserts. Clove oil is a pain reliever and disinfectant. It is of particular value in relieving teeth and gum pains. It aids digestion and is an antiflatulent.

• **Coriander *(Kusbara)*** These are round yellow granules with a particular taste. They are used to season many traditional dishes, most importantly *mulukhiyya* (green mallow). Coriander helps stimulate the secretion of gastric juices, is an antiflatulent, antispasmodic, and an appetite stimulant.

• **Cumin *(Kammun)*** Cumin has been known in Egypt since ancient times. The seeds are small, oblong granules with a hot and bitter taste. They can be used whole or ground. Cumin is a main element in fish seasoning. It is an antiflatulent, it increases digestive secretions, and helps with hyperacidity, colic, and distension.

• **Fennel *(Shamar)*** These are dry, oblong seeds containing volatile oils, which give fennel its distinctive flavor. They are used in many recipes, particularly biscuits. Fennel is used to relieve coughs, asthma, and breathing difficulties. It is also of value in treating gastric conditions, to dissolve bladder stones, and to fight harmful bacteria present in food.

• **Ginger *(Ganzabil)*** This valuable spice comes in the form of a pale yellow powder with a pungent flavor and penetrating odor. It is used either alone or in combination with cinnamon to season different foods and to flavor biscuits and desserts. It is also used as a soothing agent and has a calming effect on the stomach, is good for digestion, and is an antispasmodic, antiflatulent, and a sexual stimulant. It is drunk in the winter months as an infusion to give warmth.

• **Mastic Grains *(Mistika)*** These are pale yellow, translucent grains obtained from the resin of the mastic tree. They add a pleasant smell to meat and poultry and are a basic component of broth and soup. Mastic grains aid cases of excessive mucoid discharge as they clear the body's airways and help intestinal ulcers, colic, and gum pains.

• **Nutmeg *(Guzt al-tib)*** These aromatic, pungent seeds are large and round or oval with a grooved skin. The seeds are brown, the color of cinnamon, and are used to season meats and chickens, among others. They are ground used in combination with many other spices to make meat and fish spice. Nutmeg is a stimulant and antiflatulent. It is used as

a sexual stimulant and in the treatment of rheumatism. Excessive consumption can lead to states of agitation, nausea, and delirium.

• **Onion Seed, Fennel Flower, or Black Cumin *(Habbit al-Baraka)*** These are fine, black seeds that have an attractive smell when ground. They were known to the ancient Egyptians, and were mentioned numerous times in medical prescriptions on papyrus for the treatment of cough, chest and geriatric conditions, colds, and distension. Black cumin is ground and mixed with honey to make *mufataqa*, which is a diuretic and helps in dissolving bladder and kidney stones.

• **Pepper *(Filfil aswad)*** These are round granules with a black outer shell and a hot, piquant taste. When finely ground with the shells, black pepper is the result; when ground without the shells, white pepper results.

• **Pepper (Red)/Hot cayenne or chili powder *(Filfil ahmar or Shatta)*** This pod (unrelated to black pepper) has a characteristically spicy taste that burns the tongue. It contains vitamin C and volatile oils. Its powder is used to stimulate the appetite and the secretion of gastric juices. It is also used as a component of ointments used in the treatment of rheumatism and joint inflammations.

15

- **Rosemary (Hassa liban)** This comes in powder form or dried leaves. It has a camphor-like smell. Rosemary is generally used to season fish and meat. Because of its bactericidal and fungicidal properties, it is also used to preserve some foodstuffs stored for long durations. It treats biliary diseases, raising low blood pressure and improving the circulation.
- **Turmeric (Karkam)** This is a dark yellow powder with a strong pungent flavor. Small amounts are sufficient to give its deep color and flavor to any food in which it is used. It is particularly favored in certain rice and meat dishes. Turmeric can inhibit the growth of tumors in the body by preventing malignant cell division. It is also helpful in cases of pain and colic.
- **Salt (Malh)** There are several types of salt; finely ground salt is used at the table, while coarsely ground salt is used for cooking and salting. There is salt with added iodine and 'light' salt for cardiac and hypertensive patients. Adults require about 3.8 grams a day.
- **Spice, Mixed (Buharat)** This is a mixture of many different spices such as black peppercorns, nutmeg, cumin, cinnamon, cloves, and bay leaves. Small amounts should be ground and used as soon as possible when the flavor is still fresh. Mixed spices are used to season meat, fish, and poultry.
- **Thyme (Za'tar)** Thyme is one of the most effective plants that aid the digestion of heavy foods. It is usually added to meats along with vinegar or lime juice to soften the meat. Thyme is an antiflatulent, antispasmodic, and purifier of the stomach, liver, and chest. It is also a diuretic. Thyme is used in seasoning fish and along with salt, cumin, and other spices in making thyme *duqqa*, an appetite stimulant that is added to boiled eggs, soft cheese, or eaten with certain types of bread. For duqqa ingredients and method see page 223.

17

Fresh Herbs and Greens

H erbs and greens add numerous nutritional values to food as well as flavor variety. It is preferable to use herbs fresh and not to store them for too long to preserve their effectiveness. Fresh herbs are readily available all year round at relatively low prices. They can be added to most foods as a garnish. Even adding just a handful of chopped parsley to a soup, for example, will have a large impact on the dish's taste and health-giving attributes.

- **Celery *(Karafs)*** Celery has been known since pharaonic times for its value as a sexual stimulant, diuretic, fever reliever, and the treatment of nervous breakdowns. It is used as an appetite stimulant, for kidney and digestive disturbances and to counter-act obesity. It is used in the preparation of soups and seafood casseroles.

- **Chard *(Silq)*** Chard has broad green leaves and thick hollow stems. It is used in the preparation of many dishes such as colcassia and broad beans *(fuliyya)*. It has a high content of vitamins A and C and important mineral salts such as iron. It also has laxative properties. Chard is an anti-spasmodic for the colon and prevents the formation of excess gases in the stomach and intestines.

- **Chickpeas *(Hummus akhdar or Malana)*** Known since the time of the ancient Egyptians, they are eaten either in their fresh state or as dried seeds (local chickpeas). They contain calcium and phosphorous as well as a little oxalic acid. Chickpeas are considered to be a diuretic and stimulant of sexual desire and seminal fluid formation.

- **Chicory *(Shikuria or Siris)*** Known since pharaonic times, chicory was called "friend of the liver." It was used by the Greeks to cleanse the liver in cases of poisoning, to treat jaundice, inflammations and allergies, and eye fatigue.

- **Coriander *(Kusbara)*** It is a green herb with leaves similar to those of parsley but larger and with serrated edges. Coriander has a strong taste and is fried with garlic to form the taqliya for colcassia. It is also one of the greens used for stuffing vegetables and in soups. It is considered an antiflatulent, antispasmodic, and appetite stimulant.

- **Dill *(Shabat)*** Dill is another one of the herbs known to ancient Egyptians and is characterized by its penetrating smell. It contains antiseptic and antispasmodic substances and helps relieve gastric pains. It also stimulates the release of milk in lactating women.

- **Leek *(Kurat)*** Leeks resemble the stems of green onions, although a particular variety (*Allium porrum*) do not have the white heads. They are used in many foods, particularly with fish and are a component of the falafil mix. Leeks have health benefits similar to those of onions. In the ancient world, the Greek historian Pliny wrote that the best leeks came from Egypt, and also, remains of leeks have been found in tombs dating from 1550-1320 B.C.

- **Lettuce *(Khass)*** Known to the ancient Egyptians as a symbol of the god of fertility, lettuce contains vitamins A and E which are of multiple benefits to sexual functions and aid infertility, particularly among males. Lettuce helps calm nerves, treat insomnia, support the liver, and treat atherosclerosis. It is also a natural diuretic and laxative.

- **Mint *(Na'na')*** Mint is one of the most commonly used herbs due to its special taste and odor. It can be added to many dishes. It aids digestion, bile secretion, and is an antispasmodic and antiflatulent. It can be added to tea or used alone as either a cold or hot drink.

- **Onions, Green *(Basal akhdar)*** Also known as spring onions, these are onion buds with long, thin stems, which are both eaten. Known since the time of the ancient Egyptians, green onions (and lentils) were mentioned by Greek historian Herodotus as part of the daily diet of the workers who built the pyramids. Along with bread and cheese, they have also long been a staple food of the Egyptian farmer. Green onions are an appetite stimulant, disinfectant, bactericidal, stimulant of bile secretions, and expectorant. They are also believed to help in the treatment of hypertension, diabetes, intestinal worms, sexual weakness and asthma. Green onions also aid sleep.

- **Parsley *(Baqdunis)*** Parsley has great nutritional value due to its high content of important minerals such as iron, calcium, magnesium, and vitamin A. It is one of the herbs richest in vitamin C, having more vitamin C per 100 grams than 100 grams of orange does. On the first day it is picked, parsley contains 240 mg of vitamin C, which decreases quickly to 30 mg on the second day. Parsley also helps digestion, and is an antiflatulent and mild diuretic.

Kitchen Equipment and Utensils

In ancient Egypt, earthenware containers were used for cooking food. These same containers, known as *bram*, are still used today. Their traditional form is unglazed, but modern bram are sometimes glazed. Lead glazes can be poisonous, however, so it is advisable to avoid glazed bram altogether.

Until recently, Egyptians also used copper utensils lined with tin for cooking. More recently, cookware made of aluminum, Teflon, and stainless steel has been more popular. To decide which type of cooking utensil to use, a comparison must be made among the different kinds now available on the market.

Types of Cooking Utensils

• **Aluminum** utensils are strong, durable, not easily scratched, and relatively easy to clean. They are good conductors of heat, transmitting and holding it well. However, they may interact with some acidic foods and some egg dishes that are prepared over very low heat. Aluminum utensils are not preferred for daily cooking as studies have proven that they cause toxic precipitates in the blood.

• **Teflon** utensils make excellent cookware, particularly for frying, as the nonstick substance that coats them retains heat well, giving food the desired golden brown color. They are also easy to clean. When cooking, use only nonmetal spoons, spatulas, and stirrers to avoid scratching the nonstick coating. Before the first use, wipe Teflon utensils with a piece of cloth or a paper towel saturated with a few drops of oil.

• **Copper** utensils are among the best types of cookware, as they both acquire and lose heat quickly, thus allowing excellent control while cooking. However, they are difficult to care for, requiring special cleaning and retinning of the surfaces touching the food, as copper is toxic. They also require frequent polishing, which can be done with half a lemon dipped in salt, or commercial copper polish. Acidic foods are best not prepared in copper utensils as they interact to produce a poisonous green substance called verdigris.

- **Enamel-coated** utensils are considered good cookware as they retain heat for a long time. This, however, makes them unsuitable for the cooking of rice or pasta. As the enamel can easily be scratched by a metal spoon, enameled utensils require careful handling and the use of plastic or wooden spoons.

- **Stainless steel** utensils are also among the best types of cookware as they are easily cleaned and not easily scratched. As stainless steel is not a good heat conductor, a layer of either aluminum, copper or both is added to the bottom for better heat conduction. Stainless steel utensils are highly durable and can last for life.

- **Glass or porcelain** cookware is suitable when slow cooking by indirect heat is required. Cookware of these two materials is used only for oven cooking and cannot be set directly on the flame. They are both easy to clean.

- **Earthenware** pots *(bram)* are considered an excellent choice for oven cooking as they give food a distinctive flavor. However, they are very fragile and break easily. Earthenware cookware has been used since the times of the ancient Egyptians.

To set up a kitchen suitable for the preparation of everyday meals, certain equipment is essential:

- Cooking pots and saucepans of different sizes, either aluminum or stainless steel
- An assortment of round and rectangular aluminum or Teflon pans
- Earthenware containers *(bram)* of different sizes to hold either main or side dishes. These can be used for both cooking and serving
- Teflon skillets of different sizes (small, medium, large)
- A copper skillet for deep frying
- An enameled water boiler
- A pressure cooker for emergency cooking or for foods requiring prolonged cooking
- Assorted cake and jelly molds
- A metal sifter for sifting flour
- A widely perforated metal sieve or colander for making couscous
- A manual or electric meat grinder for making kufta, falafil, and cookies
- A manual vegetable mill. This is a handle attached to a disc that is rotated to compress and grind vegetables between the disc and the perforated bottom. For example, a tomato can be pureed while the seeds and peel are separated out.
- An electric mixer for beating eggs and kneading dough

- A wire hand whisk
- A brass mortar and pestle
- A food processor
- A set of plastic mixing bowls for beating eggs and kneading dough
- An electric blender
- A couscous pot with a perforated basket that can hold food above boiling water; it can also be used to steam vegetables.

Other tools that are also important in the processes of food preparation are:

- A small kitchen scale
- Measuring cups and spoons
- A can opener, preferably the butterfly-shaped manual type
- A jar and bottle opener

- A pair of strong kitchen shears
- A set of cooking spoons hanging on a wall near the food preparation area: a ladle, a long-handled spoon, a long-handled fork, and a long-handled slotted spoon
- An assortment of plastic spoons for stirring food in Teflon or enamelled cookware
- A metal colander with tripod feet and wooden handles
- A set of different-sized, handled strainers ranging from a small one for tea to a large one for pasta
- A long-handled slotted spoon for deep frying to drain excess oil from the frying food

- A spatula for flipping meat or fish during deep frying
- A set of sharp kitchen knives in assorted sizes
- A sharpening steel for the regular sharpening of knives
- Different-sized butcher knives for cutting through bone and large pieces of meat and fish
- Knives with serrated blades for cutting bread and finely chopping vegetables
- A plastic cutting board for chopping vegetables
- A *mulukhiyya* chopper *(makhrata)*
- An onion grater
- A vegetable peeler
- A garlic crusher
- A vegetable corer with a wooden handle, used mainly for coring eggplants and zucchini
- A set of assorted serving spoons
- A small saw for sawing through.bone
- A wooden rolling pin
- A pastry brush
- A hand-held lime press
- A heavy wooden mallet for pounding meat

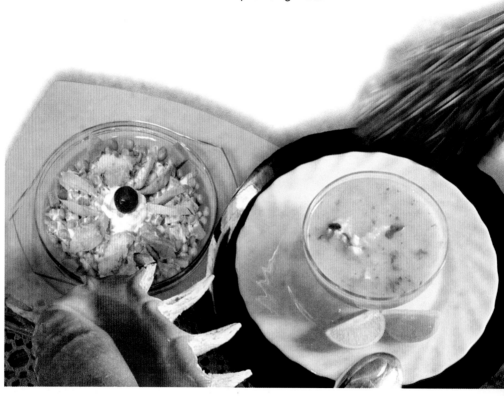

Note on the Recipes in this Book

ll the recipes in this book serve 3–4 people unless stated otherwise.

All references to 'meat' are to beef unless stated otherwise.

Soups and Broths

Soups are foods of high nutritional value as they contain important vitamins and minerals. They have a warming and comforting effect and are also believed to stimulate the release of digestives juices from the stomach. Soups are usually used as appetizers before main courses. Sometimes, when they include meat, chicken, vegetables, legumes, grains, noodles, or fried bread cubes, they can be considered a main course. Soups are a preferred dish for children, the elderly, and those who are sick or in convalescence because they are easy to digest and are so restorative. Broths are the base from which different types of soups are prepared. They can also be used instead of water in the preparation of other dishes to increase their flavor and nutrition. Broth can be prepared from chicken bones left over from boning chicken, soup bones, lamb or veal shanks or any other part of the animal. To extract broth from bones, soak the bones first in cold water for 15 minutes, then strain. Place the bones in a large pot and cover with cold water and a little salt. Bring to a boil. Using a large spoon, remove any froth that forms. Reduce heat, partially cover pot to avoid boiling over and allow broth to simmer for 3–4 hours. Add mastic grains, cardamom seeds, whole black peppercorns, a bay leaf, and a bunch of broth greens consisting of celery, leeks and carrots, which give the broth its clear golden color. Strain the broth through a cheesecloth-lined sieve, then store in the refrigerator for up to four days.

Beef Broth

Ingredients

1/2 kilogram beef
1/2 kilogram soup beef
  bones or 1 kilogram
  lamb neck (meat with
  bones)
2 liters water
1 onion
1 bunch broth greens
  (a mix of celery, leeks,
  and carrots)
3–4 mastic grains
3–4 cardamom pods
3–4 peppercorns
Bay leaf
Salt
2 tablespoons vermicelli
1 tablespoon ghee

Method

1. Rinse the meat and cut it into cubes. Soak the bones for 15 minutes, rinse, then place in a large pot with the meat. Cover meat and bones with cold water and heat to boiling.

2. Skim froth as soon as it forms. Tie onion and broth greens together or wrap in a clean cheesecloth. Add to soup.

3. Add mastic grains, cardamom, peppercorns, and bay leaf.

4. Partially cover the boiling soup to allow steam to escape. Simmer for about 30 minutes.

5. When the meat is fully cooked, add salt and strain. Return meat cubes to broth.

6. Fry the vermicelli in ghee and add to broth. Boil for 5 minutes or until vermicelli is tender. Serve hot.

Chicken Broth

Ingredients

1 medium-sized chicken
1 liter water
1 onion
1 bunch broth greens
   (a small bunch each of
   celery, leeks, carrots)
3–4 mastic grains
3–4 cardamom pods
3–4 peppercorns
Bay leaf
Salt

Method

1. Wash the chicken well, carefully removing any blood clots from within the cavity.

2. Boil water. Tie up chicken and place in boiling water along with onion and broth greens. Skim froth as it forms.

3. Add mastic grains, cardamom, pepper-corns, and bay leaf.

4. Poke thick parts of chicken breast with the tip of a knife to get rid of the blood near the bones.

5. Simmer for 30 minutes. Add salt, strain and serve.

Bone and Vegetable Soup

Method

1. Soak bones in cold water for 15 minutes, then drain. Cover with fresh cold water and bring to a boil.

2. Skim froth as soon as it forms. Add onion, mastic grains, cardamom, peppercorns, and bay leaf and reduce to a simmer.

3. Cube vegetables and rinse. Set aside.

4. After about 30 minutes, remove broth from heat. Add salt, then strain.

5. Return to heat, add zucchini, carrots, and green beans, and bring to a boil. Add potatoes 10 minutes after the other vegetables.

6. Immerse tomatoes in hot water for 1 minute, then rinse with cold water. Peel, cube, remove seeds and add to soup. Boil another 10 minutes.

Ingredients
1/2 kilogram chopped soup beef bones
1 liter water
1 onion
3–4 mastic grains
3–4 cardamom pods
3–4 peppercorns
Bay leaf
2 zucchini
2 carrots
1/4 kilogram chopped green beans or peas (shelled)
2 potatoes
2 tomatoes
1 bunch celery
Salt
Lime halves, optional
Cooked cubes of meat, optional

7. Wash celery, chop it finely and add to soup near the end of the cooking time. Remove from heat. Serve hot with lime halves if desired.

8. Boiled meat cubes can be added to the soup to increase its nutritional value.

Strained Vegetable Soup

Ingredients

4 tomatoes
2 carrots
2 large onions
2 zucchini
2 potatoes
1 sweet pepper
1 liter chicken or meat
   broth
1 tablespoon ghee
3–4 mastic grains
3–4 cardamom pods
3–4 peppercorns
Salt
Squares of pita bread
   sauted in 1 tablespoon
   ghee

Method

1. Wash and cube vegetables. Add them to broth and boil for 15 minutes.

2. Remove from heat and cool slightly. Puree in blender.

3. Heat ghee. Add mastic grains, cardamom, and peppercorns. Add pureed vegetables.

4. Boil for 5 minutes, then add a little salt. Serve hot. May be served with fried bread squares.

Tomato Soup

Ingredients

1/2 kilogram ripe tomatoes
1/4 kilogram onions
1 liter meat broth
1 tablespoon ghee
3–4 mastic grains
3–4 peppercorns
Salt
4 tablespoons fresh cream
Squares of pita bread
   sauted in 1 tablespoon
   ghee

Method

1. Cut tomatoes and onions into quarters.

   Cover with broth. Bring to a boil, then simmer for 15 minutes. Strain through a sieve, reserving vegetables.

2. Heat ghee. Add mastic grains, peppercorns, strained tomatoes, onions, and salt. Boil for 5 minutes. If needed, add some extra broth.

3. Add fresh cream and serve hot with fried-bread squares.

Tomato Soup

Ingredients
2 tablespoons ghee
2 tablespoons flour
1 tablespoon tomato paste
1 liter chicken or meat broth
Salt and pepper

Method

1. Melt ghee, stir in flour and cook until flour starts to turn yellow. Add tomato paste and stir well.

2. Add broth, salt and pepper. Boil for 10 minutes. Serve hot.

Shank Soup

Ingredients
1 beef shank
2 liters water
1 onion
3–4 mastic grains
3–4 cardamom pods
3–4 peppercorns
Bay leaf
Salt

Method

1. Clean the shank well, removing any hair. Chop and soak in cold water for 15 minutes, then rinse.

2. Boil water, then add shank. Skim froth as it forms.

3. Add onion, mastic grains, cardamom, peppercorns, and bay leaf. Simmer for 2 hours.

4. Remove from heat and set aside for 5–7 hours in the refrigerator.

5. Return to heat. Add salt and simmer for another hour.

6. Strain soup, add boiled shank, cut up into cubes with the bones, and serve hot.

Note: It is preferable to start preparing the soup the evening before serving, to allow the shank to sit in the soup all night and continue cooking in the morning.

Boiled Tripe Soup

Ingredients

1 kilogram beef tripe
1 bunch broth greens
   (a mix of celery, leeks,
   and carrots)
Bay leaf
1 onion
3–4 mastic grains
3–4 cardamom pods
3–4 peppercorns
Salt

Method

1. Clean the tripe well, first by soaking it in hot water for one to two minutes. Then spread it on a table and rub it firmly with a knife edge until it turns white. One tablespoon of bicarbonate of soda can be added to the hot water to help whiten the tripe.

2. Spread tripe and place broth greens and bay leaf inside. Roll, then tie carefully so that the tripe holds its shape.

3. Boil water and add tripe, removing froth as it forms.

4. Add onion, mastic grains, cardamom, and peppercorns. Simmer for at least 2 hours.

5. Add salt and simmer 5 more minutes. Remove from heat and strain, discarding greens and bay leaf.

6. Untie tripe. Cut into cubes and return to soup. Serve hot.

Bean Sprout Soup

Ingredients
1 tablespoon corn oil
3–4 mastic grains
1 onion
2 liters water
1/2 kilogram bean sprouts
Salt and pepper
3–4 grams cumin
Lime juice

Method

1. Heat oil. Add mastic grains, onion, then water, and bring to a boil.

2. Add bean sprouts and continue boiling, adding a little salt, pepper, and cumin. Simmer for half an hour.

3. Add lime juice. Serve.

Yellow Lentil Soup

Ingredients
1/2 kilogram yellow lentils
1 tomato, chopped into four quarters
1 potato, chopped into four quarters
1 carrot, chopped into four quarters
1 teaspoon salt
1 large onion
1 tablespoon corn oil
1 cup meat broth
1 teaspoon cumin
1 tablespoon chopped parsley
Squares of pita bread sauted in 1 tablespoon ghee

Method

1. Wash lentils well. Cover with water. Add tomato, potato, carrot, and salt and bring to a boil. Simmer for half an hour, skimming any froth that forms.

2. Remove from heat. Strain using a vegetable strainer or puree in a blender.

3. Chop onion and fry in oil until golden. Add strained lentils, broth, and cumin and simmer for l0 minutes.

4. Garnish with chopped parsley and serve hot with fried bread squares.

Crushed Broad Bean Soup

Ingredients

1/4 kilogram crushed dry
   broad beans
2 onions
Bay leaf
1 bunch celery, white part
2 tablespoons ghee
2 cups chicken or meat
   broth
4 tablespoons fresh cream
1 tablespoon butter
Pita bread squares fried
   in ghee

Method

1. Wash crushed beans
   well until water runs
   clear.

2. Cover with water and
   bring to a boil. Remove
   any froth that forms.

3. Slice 1 onion and add
   to boiling broth along
   with bay leaf and celery.
   Cover and simmer
   without stirring until
   beans are completely
   cooked. Strain.

4. Chop the second onion
   and fry in ghee until
   wilted. Add to beans.
   Add broth and boil for
   10 minutes.

5. Remove any froth that
   forms. Add extra broth
   if needed.

6. Add cream and butter.
   Serve hot with fried
   bread squares.

Cauliflower Cream Soup

Ingredients

2 tablespoons ghee
2 tablespoons flour
1 liter meat broth
Salt and pepper
1 cup cauliflower florets,
    boiled
2 tablespoons fresh cream
Squares of pita bread
    sauted in 1 tablespoon
    ghee

Method

1. Melt ghee. Stir flour in
   ghee and cook until
   flour turns yellow. Add
   broth and bring to a
   boil.

2. Add salt, pepper, and
   boiled cauliflower
   pieces. Boil for 10
   minutes.

3. Add fresh cream and
   serve hot.

Chicken Cream Soup

Ingredients

2 tablespoons flour
2 tablespoons ghee
1 liter chicken or meat
    broth
Salt and pepper
1/2 boiled chicken,
    boned and cubed
2 tablespoons fresh
    cream

Method

1. Cook flour in ghee
   until yellow in color.
   Add broth, stirring
   constantly. Add salt
   and pepper and bring
   to a boil. Reduce heat
   and simmer for 10
   minutes.

2. Add cooked chicken
   meat.

3. Remove from heat.
   Stir in fresh cream and
   serve hot.

Note: When making cream
soups, milk may be used
instead of or along with broth
to give the soup its creamy
color. Different types of cream
soups can be made using
vegetables such as
artichokes or peas.

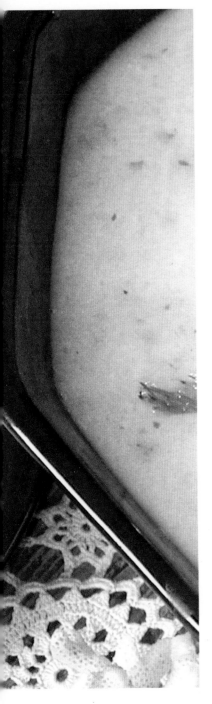

Fish Soup

Method

1. Heat oil. Fry whole onion until golden yellow. Add mastic grains, salt, and pepper.

2. Add water and bring to a boil. Wash the fish well and add it. Skim froth as it forms.

3. Add lime juice and simmer for 10 minutes.

4. Remove fish and place in a covered container.

5. Strain soup. Dissolve flour in water and add to soup through a sieve, stirring constantly until soup thickens.

6. Add parsley and boil for another 5 minutes.

7. Remove skin and bones from the fish, and cut the flesh into bite-sized chunks. Add to soup and serve hot.

Ingredients

2 tablespoons corn oil
1 small onion, whole
3–4 mastic grains
Salt and pepper
1 liter water
1 kilogram perch or bass, whole
Juice of 4 limes
2 tablespoons flour
1/2 small cup cold water to dissolve flour
2 tablespoons chopped parsley

Vegetables

egetables are of great importance in human nutrition, as they are the body's main source of minerals and vitamins, which are essential components in tissue and bone structure as well for various biological processes. Vitamins and minerals also protect the body against disease.

Vegetables are classified into several groups

Roots and Tubers

Potatoes, sweet potatoes, colcassia, onions, garlic, carrots, turnips, beets, and radishes.

- **Beets** A biennial garden plant with thick, long-stalked edible leaves and a swollen root used as vegetables or as a source of sugar. Buy small beets with the leaves still on the stalk.
- **Carrots** are among the oldest vegetables known to man for their beneficial effect upon bone illnesses. There are two types of carrots: orange and red, the orange being the more common. They are high in nutrition, providing the body with vitamins A, B, and C in the form of carotene, which is converted in the body to vitamin A. Carrots also contain iron, calcium, and potassium, which protect the body against diseases, regulate gastrointestinal functioning, and cleanse the gut of putrefied food residues. They are also helpful in cases of anaemia and thyroid disorders.
- **Colcassia (also Taro)** is a tuber with a corm and leaves, not unlike a potato with a rough outer skin; it is thought to be one of the oldest cultivated vegetables. The main food is the corm, but the leaves are also consumed, and the starch of the colcassia corm (*qulqas* in Arabic) is used to impart substance to meals.
- **Garlic** contains organic sulfur compounds, vitamins A, B complex, and C as well as hormone-like agents. It works as an antiflatulent and inhibits the growth of bacteria, fungi, and worms. It also lowers blood pressure, increases bile secretion and is of value in treating contagious

43

infections, bronchitis, and common colds. Buy garlic bulbs that are firm with tight, dry skin.

- **Onions** are also a part of many recipes, adding many health benefits to dishes. Onions have a role in the treatment of blood pressure, acne, diabetes, bronchial asthma, and intestinal worms. They also promote expectoration, improve sexual performance, and aid sleep.

- **Potatoes** are the most popular and most commonly used tuber. They are a component of many dishes and are also used as a side dish for various foods. They can be served in many forms: boiled, stewed, French-fried, or thinly sliced and deep fried to make chips, a children's favorite. Potatoes can even be served as a salad.

- **Radishes** are one of the best leafy vegetables in terms of chemical content. The radish's sharp taste and distinctive smell helps prevent the growth of oral bacteria and dental caries. Radishes also protect from heart attacks and biliary stones, and are rich in iodine, vitamin A, calcium, phosphorous, and potassium. In Egypt, people are accustomed to eating them with cheese and colcassia.

- **Sweet Potatoes** A vegetable crop, edible as a starchy tuber. It can be simmered, grilled, or baked. In Egypt it is used mainly in desserts.

- **Turnips** A herb of the mustard family with thick roots, eaten as a vegetable. Young turnips are pickled.

Leafy Vegetables and Seeds

Cabbage, green mallow (*mulukhiyya*), spinach, lettuce, purslane, mallow (*khubayza*), artichokes, peas, green beans, and broad beans.

- **Artichokes** were known to the ancient Egyptians. Artichoke hearts are available frozen in most grocery stores and supermarket outlets in Egypt. They are useful for stimulating liver functions, bile secretion and for treating cases of gout, rheumatism, and bronchial asthma.

- **Broad Beans** The seeds or pods of a climbing leguminous plant, broad beans are widely used in Egyptian cooking.

- **Cabbage** contains many vital elements such as vitamin C in large amounts, vitamin B complex, vitamin K (which protects the body from excessive bleeding), and vitamin A. Cabbage is also an important source of minerals such as calcium, magnesium, sulfur, and zinc. White cabbage with loose leaves is used widely throughout Egypt and the rest of the Middle East for stuffing.

- **Green Beans** are used widely in Egyptian cooking and are easily available in most grocers and supermarkets.
- **Green Mallow (Mulukhiyya)** There are two types of green mallow. One has a long stem and large leaves, and the other a short stem and small leaves (mint-like *mulukhiyya*). They can be cooked in the same way.
- **Lettuce** was known to the ancient Egyptians as a symbol of the god of fertility. Lettuce contains vitamins A and E, which are good for calming nerves, helping with insomnia, improving sexual ability, treating infertility, improving liver functions, and increasing urine formation. Lettuce is a natural laxative and helps in cases of atherosclerosis, general weakness, geriatric problems, and male infertility. Romaine lettuce is the type of lettuce widely used in Egypt.
- **Mallow (Khubayza)** is a herb with lobed leaves and usually showy flowers. The leaves are the part used in cooking.
- **Peas** are a popular vegetable in Egyptian cooking, often used in stews.
- **Purslane** is a fleshy-leaved trailing plant with tiny bright yellow flowers. It can be a troublesome weed but is also grown as a pot herb and used in salads or cooked.

- **Spinach** is one of the most important leafy vegetables, as it is rich in chlorophyll, proteins, and minerals such as iron, magnesium, phosphates, and iodine. Therefore, it aids digestion and stimulates the secretion of many digestive juices from the stomach, liver, and pancreas. It is recommended for growing children and adolescents, for the sick and those in convalescence, and for those suffering from anaemia, general weakness, and loss of memory. It also acts as a stimulant for new red cell synthesis in cases of rapid cell oxidation. It is cooked in stews and used as a stuffing for savory pastries. It is available both fresh and frozen.

Other Types of Vegetables

Cucumbers, tomatoes, okra, sweet peppers, eggplants, zucchini, and pumpkin.
- **Cucumbers** are highly nutritious, and are usually eaten fresh rather than cooked. They have been known to man for a long time. Cucumbers are high in vitamins, particularly vitamins A and B. They are rich in important minerals such as calcium, sodium, and magnesium. They are considered a laxative and a diuretic, helping rid the body of excess water and therefore are of value in cardiac and renal diseases. Cucumbers also help dissolve the build-up of urates

in the body. In Egypt and the Middle-East, cucumbers are small and thin, unlike the type found in Europe and North America.

• **Eggplants** *(rumi and 'arus)* A widely cultivated perennial herb that is related to the potato and yields edible fruit. It is usually a smooth and purple ovoid-shaped fruit. In Egypt there are two types of eggplant available for cooking, the large eggplant (called *rumi*), which is always purple, and the thin, more oval-shaped kind (called *'arus*), which is usually stuffed and cooked; this is available in both purple and white colors.

• **Okra (***bamya***)** There are three types of okra, which differ in appearance and flavor:

Falahi **(farmer)** okra is characterized by its dark green color and by the presence of fine, hairlike thorns on the sides, which must be removed during preparation. Okra is cleaned by finely peeling the ridges to remove the thorns and by turning the okra around a knife to remove the hard cap, giving it a conical shape.

Rumi **okra** has a light green color and no thorns.

Red okra which is similar to rumi okra, but has a reddish cap. The red color may extend to the pod.

Notice that when preparing Burani or Wika okra, you must select large pods with large seeds.

• **Pumpkin** Large, pulpy, deep-yellow, round fruit of the squash family. Pumpkins are used mainly in desserts in Egypt.

• **Sweet Peppers** are commonly used in salads, vegetable dishes, and pickles.

• **Tomatoes** are considered a main component of salads due to their high content of carbohydrates and important mineral salts such as iron, copper, sulfur, and potassium, phosphorous and calcium. They are also a main source of vitamins A, B, C, and D. Tomatoes are good for diabetic and hypertensive patients.

• **Zucchini** is a summer squash of bushy growth with smooth, slender cylindrical green fruits. The zucchini available in Egypt is small in size and light green in color, unlike the dark-green, larger fruits found in Europe and North America.

Advice for Buying and Cooking Vegetables

• Buy vegetables while they are in season. Avoid buying them as soon as they appear, because they tend to be expensive then.

• Choose vegetables that are firm, brightly colored, and shiny.

• Select green leafy vegetables that are deeply colored.

• Eat vegetables as fresh as possible, because as soon as they are picked, destructive enzymes begin to affect them.

• To maintain fresh vegetables as long as possible, store them in plastic bags in a cold dark place, such as the refrigerator.

• Do not store longer than one week.

• Wash vegetables under running water.

• Avoid peeling vegetables whenever possible, as many of the vitamins lie directly under the skin.

• When peeling vegetables, try removing the thinnest layer, or just scrape lightly.

• To avoid the loss of vitamins B and C, add a few drops of lemon or vinegar to the water you soak the vegetables in, as the acid helps preserve both the vitamins and the color.

• After boiling vegetables, save the vitamin-rich water for use in cooking. Do not add bicarbonate of soda to vegetables to preserve their color while cooking, as this spoils their vitamin content.

• Avoid repeated reheating of food as this decreases its nutritional value.

• Salad must be prepared as close to eating time as possible. Salt and lime juice must be added immediately before serving.

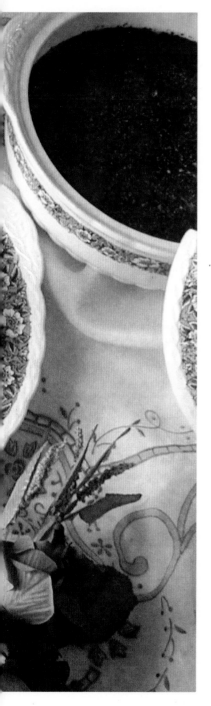

Green Mallow with Poultry

Method

1. Boil poultry in the usual way (see chicken broth page 31). Reserve 1 liter of the broth.

2. Pick off the mallow leaves, wash and dry well with a towel. Finely chop using a *mulukhiyya* chopper or place in the freezer for 30 minutes, then chop using a food processor.

3. Crush garlic, red pepper, salt, and coriander to prepare *taqliya* (garlic mix to be fried).

4. Bring the liter of strained broth to a boil. Add part of the taqliya and boil for 5 minutes.

5. Add chopped *mulukhiyya*, stirring constantly. Bring *mulukhiyya* to a boil, stir, then bring to a boil once more. Skim any froth that forms.

6. Fry remaining garlic mix *(taqliya)* in ghee until golden yellow. Add to *mulukhiyya* and serve.

Ingredients

1 large chicken or duck
1 kilogram fresh green mallow (*mulukhiyya*)

Taqliya:
4 cloves garlic
1/2 teaspoon red pepper and pinch salt
2 tablespoons dried coriander
1 tomato (optional)
2 tablespoons ghee

Note: 1. Don't stir the *mulukhiyya* for more than 5 minutes. This recipe can also be made with rabbit.

2. You may also add a tomato to the broth, first by adding it whole to the broth for just five minutes, then straining it and adding it back to the broth.

Green Mallow Egyptian-style
(Mulukhiyya burani)

Ingredients

1 kilogram fresh green
  mallow *(mulukhiyya)*
2 tablespoons ghee
1 onion
1/2 kilogram meat, cubed
  (beef or lamb)
1 liter meat broth
Salt and pepper
1/2 cup dried chickpeas,
  soaked in water for
  1 hour

Taqliya:
4 cloves garlic
1/2 teaspoon red pepper
2 tablespoons dried
  coriander
1 tablespoon ghee

Method

1. Wash *mulukhiyya* leaves well, and dry. Fry in 1 tablespoon ghee over medium heat until leaves wilt while still maintaining their green color. Remove *mulukhiyya* and place in a sieve. Grind into a fine pulp using a *mifrak* or a mortar and pestle.

2. Grate onion and fry in 1 tablespoon ghee until golden yellow. Add meat cubes and fry, stirring occasionally. Add meat broth, salt, and pepper and simmer over low heat.

3. Before meat is fully cooked, add chickpeas, then add mulukhiyya and boil for 10 minutes.

4. Fry *taqliya* ingredients in 1 tablespoon ghee. Add to *mulukhiyya* and serve.

Note: A *mifrak* is a container similar to a brass mortar and pestle. It is made of wood and has a long wooden handle that ends in a sharp crescent-shaped knife. The *mulukhiyya* is placed in the container and the handle is placed between the palms of the hands while the knife is placed inside the container. The handle is rhythmically twisted from side to side so as to chop in a way similar to the action of an electric blender. This appliance has been in use in Egypt since early times and is still found in Upper Egypt. Today food processors are used to chop the *mulukhiyya*.

Green Mallow with Lamb

Ingredients

1 kilogram lamb meat
  with bones (neck or
  loin chops)
2 onions
Salt and pepper
1 kilogram fresh green
  mallow, (mulukhiyya),
  finely chopped

Taqliya:
4 cloves garlic
1/2 teaspoon red pepper
2 tablespoons dried
  coriander
2 tablespoons ghee

Method

1. Boil meat in the usual way (see meat broth, page 30), then strain.

2. Chop onions and add salt and pepper. Add to meat broth and simmer for about 10 minutes.

3. Add chopped *mulukhiyya*, stirring constantly. Bring *mulukhiyya* to a boil twice, skimming froth. Remove from heat.

4. Crush garlic, red pepper, and coriander to prepare *taqliya* and fry in ghee until golden yellow. Add to *mulukhiyya*.

5. Meat may be placed in a separate dish and served beside the *mulukhiyya* or may be served in the same dish as the *mulukhiyya*.

Dried Green Mallow

Ingredients

1 cup dried green mallow
  (mulukhiyya)
1 bunch each chard and
  fresh coriander
1 liter meat or chicken
  broth

Taqliya:
4 cloves garlic
1/2 teaspoon red pepper
2 tablespoons dried
  coriander
1 tablespoon ghee

Method

1. Wash *mulukhiyya*, running water over it in a fine metal sieve to get rid of any dust.

2. Wash chard and fresh coriander leaves. Finely chop using a *makhrata* or food processor. Add to *mulukhiyya* and mix well together.

3. Crush garlic, red pepper, and coriander to prepare taqliya.

4. Bring broth to a boil, add half the *taqliya* mixture and simmer for 5 minutes.

5. Add *mulukhiyya*, chard, and coriander mixture, stirring constantly. Bring to a boil twice, skimming any froth that forms. Remove from heat.

6. Fry remaining *taqliya* in ghee until golden yellow. Add to *mulukhiyya* and serve hot.

Stewed Okra with Lamb

Ingredients

1 kilogram fresh okra
1 onion
2 tablespoons ghee
1/2 kilogram lamb meat
  (loin chops)
Pepper
1 cup tomato sauce
1 liter meat broth
Salt and pepper
1 tablespoon lime juice
2 cloves garlic, chopped
1 hot chili pepper, whole

Method

1. Wash okra. Place in a sieve and dry. Remove caps and thorns.

2. Grate onion and saute in ghee until golden yellow. Rinse meat, add to onion, and stir, adding a little pepper.

3. Add tomato sauce and simmer until sauce thickens and ghee rises to top. Add broth and bring to a boil. Add salt.

4. Add okra and lime juice and boil for 10 minutes. Lower heat and simmer for about 30 minutes until ghee rises to the top and okra is well cooked.

5. Crush garlic and chop hot chili pepper. Add to okra. Serve.

Okra Casserole (Diqqiyat bamya)

Ingredients

1 kilogram fresh okra
2 tablespoons ghee
1 onion
1/2 kilogram meat, cubed
  (beef or lamb)
2 cloves garlic
1 cup tomato juice
Salt and pepper
1 cup meat broth
Juice of 1 lime
Waxed paper

Method

1. Wash okra and place in a sieve to dry. Remove caps and thorns.

2. Lightly saute okra in 1 tablespoon ghee, then drain and set aside.

3. Grate the onion, and saute it in 1 tablespoon ghee until golden yellow. Add meat, and stir occasionally. Crush the garlic, and add it.

4. Add tomato juice, salt, and pepper. Simmer until tomato sauce thickens and ghee rises to top, stirring occasionally.

5. In an earthenware container, place cooked meat cubes followed by okra arranged in layers. Add the tomato sauce that the meat was cooked in, one cup broth, and the lime juice. Cover with waxed paper. Punch a hole in the waxed paper.

6. Place in a hot oven. Check from time to time and add extra broth if needed. Bake until ghee appears on the top.

7. Place on a plate and serve hot.

Okra with Chard and Fresh Coriander

Ingredients
1 kilogram fresh okra
2 tablespoons ghee
1 onion
1/2 kilogram meat, cubed (beef or lamb)
1 1/2 liters meat broth
Salt and pepper
1 tablespoon lime juice
Green *taqliya:*
1 bunch each chard and fresh coriander
4 cloves garlic
2 tablespoons ghee

Method

1. Wash okra and place in a sieve to dry. Remove caps and thorns. Saute lightly in 1 tablespoon ghee, preserving green color of okra. Remove from ghee and place in a sieve to drain excess fat.

2. Chop onion and saute 1 tablespoon ghee until golden yellow. Add meat, stirring occasionally. Add broth and salt and pepper and bring to a boil. Add okra and lime juice. Cover and simmer over low heat.

3. To make the *taqliya*, mince chard and coriander with garlic, then saute in ghee until dry. Beat to a pulp with a mortar and pestle or process in a food processor.

4. Add *taqliya* to okra and boil for 10 minutes. Serve.

Mashed Okra with Beef

Ingredients

1 kilogram large okra
3 tablespoons ghee
1 cup tomato juice
1 onion
1/2 kilogram beef, cubed
1 1/2 liters meat broth
Salt
1/4 teaspoon red pepper
1 tablespoon lime juice
4 cloves garlic
2 tablespoons dried
    coriander

Method

1. Wash okra and place in a sieve to dry. Cut up into small pieces and lightly saute in 1 tablespoon ghee. Add tomato juice and cook for a short while. Remove from sauce and drain in a sieve.

2. Grate onion and saute in 1 tablespoon ghee until golden yellow. Add beef cubes and stir a few minutes. Add broth, cover, and simmer until meat is half cooked.

3. Add okra, salt, red pepper, and lime juice and simmer over medium heat until fully cooked.

4. Mince garlic and coriander and saute in the remaining tablespoon of ghee. Sprinkle over dish. Serve.

Mashed Okra with Chicken and 'asida

Ingredients

1 kilogram large okra

2 tablespoons ghee

1 onion

1 large chicken

1 1/2 liters chicken broth

Salt and pepper

1 tablespoon lime juice

4 cloves garlic

2 tablespoons dried
    coriander

'Asida:

1 cup butter

1 liter chicken broth

Salt and pepper

1 cup flour

Method for Okra

Follow the steps for Mashed Okra with Beef, but use chicken, omit the tomato juice, and use black pepper instead of red pepper. *'Asida* is served in a separate dish beside the okra.

Method for 'asida

1. Place butter and chicken broth in a sauce pan.

Heat to boiling, add salt and pepper.

2. Add flour, stirring constantly with a spoon or a wire whisk. Cook over medium heat for about 10 minutes.

3. Pour *'asida* in a dish. Sprinkle with some of the cooked okra and serve alongside it.

Burani Okra

Ingredients

1 kilogram fresh okra

2 tablespoons ghee

1 onion

1/2 kilogram lamb meat,
    cubed

1 cup tomato juice

Salt and pepper

1 cup broth

1 tablespoon fine bread
    crumbs

Method

1. Wash, drain, and remove caps from okra. Lightly saute in 1 tablespoon ghee, then drain in a colander to get rid of excess fat.

2. Chop onion and saute in 1 tablespoon ghee until golden yellow. Add meat, stirring occasionally until meat is lightly browned.

3. Add tomato juice, salt, and pepper. Cook over medium heat until mixture boils.

4. Grease a casserole dish lightly with ghee. Arrange in layers: half the okra, then the meat cubes, then the remaining okra.

5. Pour tomato juice that the meat was cooked in and broth over okra. Place in a hot oven for about 30 minutes.

6. Sprinkle top with fine, dried bread crumbs and a little melted ghee. Bake for another 10 minutes or until top is lightly browned. Serve.

Colcassia with Chard and Fresh Coriander

Ingredients

1 kilogram colcassia

1/2 cup salt (for washing colcassia)

1/2 cup flour (for washing colcassia)

1 onion

Salt and pepper

1 1/2 liters meat broth

1/2 kilogram lamb meat

1 tablespoon lime juice

1 bunch each of fresh chard and coriander

4 large cloves garlic

1 tablespoon corn oil

Method

1. Peel colcassia and divide in half. Cut each half horizontally into thick slices. Cut slices into fingers and cut fingers into cubes.

2. Rub colcassia well with salt. Cover with hot water and soak for 10 minutes. Wash thoroughly with warm water. Dredge with flour, and rub the surfaces of the colcassia. Rinse again with warm water and continue washing until completely rid of the mucoid substance which covers colcassia.

3. Chop onion and season with salt and pepper. Rub into meat.

4. Boil broth. Add onion and meat and boil for about 30 minutes.

5. Add washed colcassia cubes to broth. Add lime juice. Cook until colcassia is soft (about 30 minutes).

6. Wash chard and coriander leaves. Mince with garlic and saute in oil. Add to colcassia and cook for 10 minutes. Serve.

Colcassia with Ground Meat

Ingredients

1 kilogram colcassia
2 tablespoons ghee
1/2 kilogram ground beef
1 1/2 cups tomato juice
Salt and pepper
1 cup meat broth

Method

1. Peel colcassia and cut into quarters. Slice into 1 cm thick triangles. Wash as described opposite (page 58). Dry well and lightly saute in ghee. Remove colcassia from pan.

2. Stir ground beef into ghee in pan. Add 1 cup tomato juice and season with salt and pepper. Cook over medium heat until well cooked.

3. Place tomato juice and meat in an earthenware dish. Arrange colcassia on top.

4. Add remaining 1/2 cup tomato juice and meat broth. Bake in an oven until sauce thickens and ghee rises to the top. To serve.

Colcassia with Tomato

Method

1. Peel and cube colcassia, and rub with the salt and wash it as described opposite (page 58). Saute in 1 tablespoon ghee. Drain.

2. Chop onion and saute in 1 tablespoon ghee until golden yellow. Add meat cubes, stirring for a few minutes. Add about 1 liter broth and bring to a boil. Reduce heat and simmer until meat is almost cooked. Add salt.

3. Add tomato juice and simmer until tomato juice thickens and ghee rises to the top.

Ingredients

1 kilogram colcassia
2 tablespoons ghee
1 onion
1/2 kilogram meat, cubed
　(beef or lamb)
1 1/2 liters meat broth
1/4 cup salt
2 cups tomato juice
4 cloves garlic
1/4 teaspoon red pepper

4. Add remaining 1/2 liter broth and boil. Add sauted colcassia cubes and cook until done (about 30 minutes).

5. Crush garlic and red pepper. Add to colcassia and boil for 10 minutes. Serve.

Fried Eggplant with Ground Meat
(Musaqqa'a)

Method

1. Partially pare egg-plants by removing lengthwise strips. Cut crossways into 1 cm thin slices.

2. Wash, add salt, and allow 15 minutes in a colander for salt to draw out excess water from eggplant pieces.

3. Pat dry and deep fry in hot oil (about 5 cm deep) until golden yellow. Place on absorbent towels.

4. Finely chop onions. Saute in ghee until golden yellow, then add ground meat. Cook over medium heat for about 10 minutes. Add salt and pepper and cook over low heat for another 10 minutes.

5. Slice garlic and saute in a little oil. Add toma-to juice and vinegar and simmer until toma-to juice thickens and oil rises to the top. Add broth and boil.

Ingredients
1 kilogram *rumi* eggplants
Oil for deep frying
2 large onions
1 tablespoon ghee
1/2 kilogram ground meat
Salt and pepper
2 cloves garlic
1 cup tomato juice
1 tablespoon vinegar
1 cup beef broth
1/2 cup small dried chick-peas, soaked in water for 1 hour

6. Arrange half the egg-plant slices in a Teflon or casserole dish. Cover with layer of ground beef. Arrange remaining eggplant on top of meat, then sprin-kle with chickpeas.

7. Pour tomato and broth mixture into baking dish and bake in a hot oven for about 30 min-utes or until juices are reduced and oil rises to the top. Serve.

Eggplants with Béchamel Sauce

Ingredients

1 kilogram small rumi
   eggplants
Oil for deep frying
1/2 kilogram cooked
   ground meat
1 egg, beaten
An egg-sized piece of
   butter

Béchamel sauce:
2 tablespoons flour
2 tablespoons ghee
2 cups milk
Salt and pepper

Method

1. Cut eggplants in half lengthwise (do not remove the stems) and deep fry in hot oil (about 5 cm deep).

2. Make béchamel sauce: Fry flour in ghee until color turns yellow. Add milk, stirring constantly until mixture thickens. Season with salt and pepper.

3. Scoop out the eggplant flesh, using a small spoon. Mix the flesh with cooked ground meat (mu'sag) and 2 tablespoons béchamel sauce. Season with salt and pepper.

4. Fill eggplant halves with the above mixture and arrange in baking dish. Cover with remaining béchamel sauce. Cover béchamel with beaten egg and butter.

5. Bake in medium hot oven until top is lightly browned. Serve.

Fried Eggplant with Béchamel Sauce
(Musaqqa'a bi-l-bashamil)

Ingredients

1 kilogram *rumi* eggplants
Oil for deep frying
1/2 kilogram cooked
  ground beef
1 egg

Béchamel sauce:
2 tablespoons flour
2 tablespoons ghee
2 cups milk
Salt and pepper

Method

1. Peel and slice egg-plants, wash, add salt, and place in colander for 15 minutes to drain excess water.

2. Deep fry in hot oil (about 5 cm deep) and place on absorbent towels.

3. Make béchamel sauce: Fry flour in ghee until color turns yellow. Add milk, stirring constantly until mixture thickens. Season with salt and pepper.

4. Arrange half the eggplant slices in a baking dish. Cover with ground beef and arrange remaining eggplant in a second layer.

5. Cover top with béchamel sauce.

6. Beat egg and coat béchamel top. Bake in a medium hot oven for about 30 minutes or until top is lightly browned. Serve.

Stewed Eggplant *(Musaqqa'a makmura)*

Ingredients
1 kilogram rumi eggplants
1 onion
Salt and pepper
1/2 kilogram tomatoes
1/2 kilogram meat, cubed (beef or lamb)
1/4 cup small dried chickpeas, soaked in hot water for 1 hour
2 tablespoons ghee

Method

1. Wash eggplants. Peel and cut into medium cubes.

2. Slice onion and combine with salt and pepper.

3. Peel tomatoes: to facilitate peeling, immerse in hot water for one minute then wash with cold water. Cut into cubes.

4. In a cooking pot, layer half the ingredients in the following order: eggplant, onion, tomato, chickpeas, then meat cubes. Repeat.

5. Add ghee to top. Cover tightly and simmer over low heat until completely cooked.

Breaded Eggplant

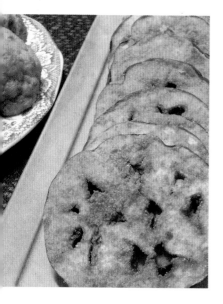

Ingredients

1 kilogram *rumi* eggplants

Salt

2 eggs

Pepper

Fine dried breadcrumbs

Oil for deep frying

Chopped parsley

Method

1. Peel eggplants and slice into slices. Wash, sprinkle with salt, and set aside in a colander for 15 minutes.

2. Beat eggs with salt and pepper. Pat eggplant slices dry, cover with beaten egg, then coat with breadcrumbs.

3. Deep fry in hot oil (about 5 cm deep). Drain on absorbent paper. Sprinkle with parsley and serve hot.

Mixed Vegetable Casserole *(Diqqiyat turli)*

Ingredients

Same ingredients as recipe for Stewed Mixed Vegetables (page 68).

Add:

1 cup tomato juice

1 tablespoon lime juice

Method

1. Clean vegetables and cut into bite-sized pieces.

2. Chop onions and saute in ghee until golden yellow. Crush the garlic, add to onions, stir, and add meat. Continue stirring.

3. Dice tomatoes. Mix well with all above ingredients.

4. Add tomato juice seasoned with salt and pepper. Continue cooking over low heat until juice thickens and ghee rises to top. Add broth and bring to a boil.

5. Arrange the prepared vegetables and meat in 4 or 5 brams, to be served as is. Pour tomato juice on top. Add lime juice and boil on stove top for a few minutes. Bake in a medium hot oven until sauce thickens and ghee rises to top, and top is lightly browned. Serve hot.

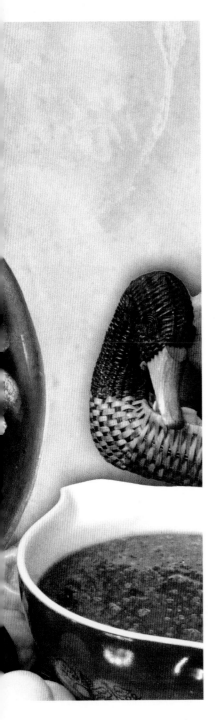

Potato and Lamb Casserole

Ingredients

1 kilogram potatoes
2 large onions
5 cloves garlic
Salt and pepper
Pinch nutmeg
1/2 kilogram lamb rib or
  loin chops
1 tomato
1 sweet pepper
1 cup tomato juice
I cup meat broth
1 tablespoon ghee

Method

1. Peel potatoes and cut into 1 cm thick slices.

2. Slice onions and garlic, add salt, pepper, and nutmeg, and rub onto meat.

3. Arrange half the potatoes and half the onion mixture in a casserole. Add meat, then cover with remaining potatoes and onions.

4. Slice tomato and pepper. Arrange on top of potatoes. Add tomato juice, meat broth, and ghee.

5. Bake in a hot oven for 1 hour. Lower heat and bake for another 30 minutes until completely cooked and top is lightly browned. Serve.

Stewed Mixed Vegetables
(Turli mishakkil makmur)

Ingredients

1/4 kilogram zucchini

1/4 kilogram rumi
eggplants

1/4 kilogram sweet
peppers

1/4 kilogram okra

1/4 kilogram green beans

2 onions

4 cloves garlic

Salt and pepper

1/2 teaspoon mixed spices

1 kilogram lamb meat,
cubed

1/2 kilogram tomatoes

1 cup meat broth

2 tablespoons ghee

Method

1. Clean vegetables and cut into bite-sized pieces.

2. Slice onions and garlic, add salt, pepper, and mixed spices and rub into meat.

3. Dice tomatoes. Mix well with all above ingredients.

4. Place the vegetables and meat in a metal baking pan. Add broth and ghee. Place on medium heat for 30 minutes, then in a medium hot oven until lightly browned and cooked. Serve hot.

Peas and Carrots with Meat

Ingredients

1 kilogram green peas
1/4 kilogram yellow
    carrots
2 cloves garlic
1 onion
Salt and pepper
1/2 kilogram meat, cubed
1 cup tomato juice
1 liter meat broth
2 tablespoons ghee

Method

1. Shell peas. Dice carrots. Slice garlic finely.

2. Chop onion and season with salt and pepper. Rub onto meat.

3. Mix all above ingredients in a large cooking pot. Add tomato juice, meat broth, and ghee. Cook over medium heat about 30 minutes. Lower and simmer for 15 minutes until sauce thickens and ghee rises to top. Serve.

Potato Wedges with Tomato Sauce

Ingredients

1 kilogram potatoes
Oil for deep frying
1 small onion, whole
1 tablespoon ghee
2 cloves garlic, whole
1/2 kilogram meat, cubed
    (beef or lamb)
1 liter meat broth
1 cup tomato juice
Salt and pepper

Method

1. Peel potatoes. Cut into thick wedges and deep fry in oil (about 5 cm deep) until a light golden color. Set aside.

2. Peel onion and saute lightly in ghee. Add garlic cloves and stir. Add the meat and half the broth. Simmer until well cooked.

3. Add tomato juice seasoned with salt and pepper. Simmer until sauce thickens and ghee rises to the top.

4. Add remaining broth and bring to a boil. Add potatoes and boil for 10 minutes. Serve

Puréed Potatoes

Ingredients

1 kilogram potatoes
2 tablespoons butter
1 cup milk
2 eggs
Salt and pepper
1/4 kilogram cooked
　　ground meat
1 egg
Pepper
1 tablespoon fine dried
　　breadcrumbs
2 tablespoons butter

Method

1. Boil potatoes in salted water until well cooked. Peel and mash with a fork.

2. Add butter, milk, eggs, salt, and pepper. Beat well with an electric mixer.

3. Grease an ovenproof dish with ghee. Spread half the potato mixture, cover with a layer of cooked ground meat (*mu'sag*), then evenly spread the remaining potato mixture.

4. Beat an egg with a little pepper and use to brush the top. Sprinkle the dried breadcrumbs and butter on the top.

5. Bake in a medium hot oven for 30 minutes until top is golden brown. Serve

Peas with Artichokes

Ingredients

Same as Peas and Carrots with Meat recipe on page 69 but replace carrots with artichoke cubes. (See how to prepare artichokes, page 77).

Spinach with Béchamel Sauce

Method

1. Chop spinach. Soak in water, then drain in a colander and wash under running water. Boil in a small amount of salted water for 10 minutes. Drain.

2. Make béchamel sauce: fry flour in ghee until yellow in color. Add milk and stir constantly until mixture thickens. Season with salt and pepper.

3. Grease baking dish. Arrange in layers half the spinach, then the cooked ground beef, then the remaining spinach.

Ingredients

1 kilogram fresh spinach
1/4 kilogram cooked
    ground beef
1 egg
Butter

Béchamel sauce:
2 tablespoons flour
2 tablespoons ghee
2 cups milk
Salt and pepper

4. Cover top with béchamel sauce. Beat egg. Brush béchamel top with egg and a little butter. Bake in a medium hot oven until lightly browned. Serve.

Stewed Spinach with Meat

Ingredients

1 kilogram fresh spinach

1 onion

2 tablespoons ghee

1/2 kilogram meat, cubed (beef or lamb)

4 cloves garlic

1 bunch fresh coriander

2 cups tomato juice

Salt and pepper

1 cup meat broth

1/4 cup small dried chickpeas, or soft rubbed grain *(firik)*, soaked in hot water for 1 hour

Method

1. Chop spinach. Soak in water, then drain in a colander and wash under running water.

2. Chop onion and saute in ghee until golden yellow. Add meat cubes and stir until liquid is partially absorbed.

3. Mince garlic and coriander, then add to meat and stir.

4. Add tomato juice seasoned with salt and pepper. Simmer until liquid is reduced and ghee rises to the top.

5. Add broth and bring to a boil. Add spinach and bring to a boil. Add chickpeas or soft rubbed grain *(firik)*.

6. Cook over medium heat for 15 minutes, then lower heat and simmer until liquid is reduced and ghee rises to the top. Serve.

Stewed Spinach

Ingredients

1 kilogram fresh spinach

2 onions

Salt and pepper

1/2 kilogram meat slices (beef or lamb)

1/2 cup small dried chick-peas or soft rubbed grain (firik), soaked in hot water for 1 hour

2 cups tomato juice

1 cup meat broth

4 cloves garlic

1 bunch fresh coriander

Salt and pepper

2 tablespoons ghee

Method

1. Chop and wash spinach as described in previous recipe.

2. Slice onions, season with salt and pepper, then rub on meat.

3. In a deep pot, arrange in layers half of spinach, onion mixture, all of meat, then remaining spinach, and onion mixture.

4. Add chickpeas or soft rubbed grain (firik).

5. Pour tomato juice and broth over spinach and cook over medium heat for 30 minutes.

6. Mince garlic and fresh coriander with a little salt and pepper. Add half the garlic mixture to the cooking spinach and meat. Saute the remaining half in ghee and toss with spinach.

7. Allow spinach to cook for 10 minutes, or until the liquid is absorbed. Serve.

Purslane with Meat

Ingredients

1 kilogram fresh purslane (regla)

1 onion

2 tablespoons ghee

1/2 kilogram meat, cubed (beef or lamb)

1/4 cup small dried chick-peas, or soft rubbed grain (firik), soaked in hot water for 1 hour

2 cups tomato juice

Salt and pepper

2 cups meat broth

4 garlic cloves

1 bunch fresh coriander

Method

1. Cut up purslane and wash well.

2. Grate onion and saute in ghee until golden yellow. Add meat and stir for two minutes. Add chickpeas or soft rubbed grain (firik) and stir for two minutes. Add tomato juice seasoned with salt and pepper. Simmer until liquid is reduced and ghee rises to the top.

3. Add broth and bring to a boil. Add purslane. Cook over medium heat for about 30 minutes.

4. Mince garlic and fresh coriander. Add half the garlic mixture to the cooking purslane. Saute the remaining half in ghee then toss on top of purslane. Boil for 10 minutes. Serve.

Mallow (Khubayza)

Ingredients

1 kilogram mallow
  (khubayza)
2 large bunches chard
1 onion
2 tablespoons ghee
1/2 kilogram meat, cubed
  (beef or lamb)
2 cups tomato juice
Salt and pepper
1 bunch fresh dill
1 bunch fresh coriander
1/2 cup soft rubbed grain
  (firik), soaked in hot
  water for 1 hour, or rice
4 cloves garlic, minced

Method

1. Pick mallow and chard leaves, and wash. Boil in a little salted water, and drain. Mix it in a mixer.

2. Chop onion. Saute lightly in 1 tablespoon ghee until golden yellow. Add meat cubes and stir.

3. Add tomato juice seasoned with salt and pepper. Chop the dill and coriander. Add mallow and half the dill and coriander mixture to tomato juice.

4. Cover and simmer. When half cooked, add grain (firik) or rice. Continue until fully cooked. (about 30 minutes).

5. Saute garlic and remaining dill and coriander in 1 tablespoon ghee. Toss onto mallow. Serve.

74

Burani Mallow

Ingredients

1 kilogram mallow
   (khubayza)
2 tablespoons ghee
1 onion
1/2 kilogram meat, cubed
   (beef or lamb)
1 liter meat broth
Salt and pepper
1 cup small dried chick-
   peas, soaked in hot
   water for 1 hour
4 cloves garlic
1 bunch fresh coriander

Method

1. Wash mallow leaves
   and pat dry. Saute
   lightly in 1 tablespoon
   ghee, then remove
   while still green in
   color.

2. Grate onion and saute
   lightly in 1 tablespoon
   ghee until golden
   yellow. Add meat and
   stir for two minutes.

3. Cover with broth and
   bring to a boil. Add salt
   and pepper and

simmer until meat is
half cooked. Add chick-
peas and mallow and
continue simmering,
stirring occasionally
until fully cooked.

4. Mince garlic and
   coriander, then add
   half the mixture to the
   cooking mallow. Saute
   the rest and add to top
   of mallow. Serve.

Stuffed Artichokes with Ground Beef

Ingredients

6 medium artichokes
2–3 limes, sliced in half
1/4 cup flour
2 onions
1 bunch parsley, dill, mint
Salt and pepper
1/2 kilogram ground beef
2 tablespoons ghee
1 cup tomato juice
1 cup water or broth

Method

1. Prepare artichokes by removing outside leaves with a paring knife and clipping the remaining tips evenly. Trim stems even with artichoke bases, and rub surfaces with the lime to prevent discoloration. Remove the fuzzy center of the artichokes using a tablespoon and discard. Rub the artichokes with lime juice. Place artichokes in a bowl of water with added lime juice and flour.

2. Mince one of the onions, parsley, dill, and mint and season well with salt and pepper. Add to ground meat.

3. Rinse artichokes. Stuff with above mixture, then arrange in an oven proof dish.

4. Grate the other onion and lightly saute in ghee until yellow. Add tomato juice and cook until sauce thickens and ghee rises to the top. Add 1 cup of water or broth and bring to a boil.

5. Pour above mixture into dish with artichokes. Bake in a medium hot oven for about 30 minutes or until artichokes are cooked and sauce is thickened. Serve.

Stewed Artichokes with Lamb

Ingredients

6 artichokes
2 tablespoons ghee
1/2 kilogram lamb meat, cubed
2 cups broth
Salt and pepper

Method

1. Prepare artichokes for cooking as described in previous recipe. Cut them into quarters.

2. Melt ghee. Add meat and stir for a few minutes. Season broth with salt and pepper and add gradually to meat. Simmer until meat is almost cooked.

3. Add quartered artichokes and cook for about 10 minutes. Shake the pot to move the pieces around while they are cooking. Do not stir with a spoon.

4. Cook over low heat until liquid is almost absorbed and flavors are blended. Serve.

Stuffed Artichokes with Béchamel Sauce

Ingredients
6 artichokes
1/2 kilogram cooked ground meat
Béchamel sauce:
2 tablespoons flour
2 tablespoons ghee
1 cup milk
Salt and pepper
White sauce:
2 tablespoons flour
2 tablespoons ghee
2 cups meat broth
Salt and pepper

Method

1. Prepare artichokes for cooking as described on page 77. Boil for 10 minutes.

2. Prepare béchamel sauce: fry flour in ghee until yellow in color, then add cold milk, salt and pepper. Stir continuously until mixture thickens.

3. Mix two tablespoons of béchamel sauce with the cooked ground meat. Stuff artichokes. Arrange in a baking pan and cover with remaining béchamel sauce.

4. Prepare white sauce: fry flour in ghee until golden in color. Add broth, salt, and pepper, stirring continuously. Pour over artichokes. Bake in medium hot oven for about 30 minutes until liquid is absorbed and top is lightly browned. Serve.

Stewed Artichokes with Fresh Broad Beans

Ingredients

6 artichokes

1 kilogram fresh broad beans (select beans that are small and have a soft shell)

1 onion

Salt and pepper

1/2 kilogram meat, cubed (beef or lamb)

1 cup tomato juice

2 tablespoons ghee

Method

1. Prepare artichokes as described on page 77. Cut into quarters.

2. Wash broad beans well. Remove stems and string-like fibers on the side. Chop into bite-sized pieces.

3. Grate onion, season with salt and pepper and rub onto meat.

4. Mix artichokes, broad beans, and meat, and place in a cooking pot. Add tomato juice and ghee, then cover. Cook over medium heat for 30 minutes. Reduce heat and simmer for 15 minutes until sauce thickens and ghee rises to top. Serve.

Artichokes and Fresh Broad Beans Cooked in Oil

Ingredients

10 artichokes

1 onion

White upper part of 1
  celery stick

1 carrot

1/2 cup oil

1 liter water

Juice of 2 limes

1 kilogram fresh broad
  beans, shelled

1 bunch dill

Method

1. Prepare artichokes as described on page 77. Partially cook in boiling water.

2. Mince onion, celery, and carrot. Saute lightly in oil, preserving colors of vegetables.

3. Add 1 liter water and bring to a boil, then add artichokes and lime juice. Cover. Cook over medium heat until half cooked.

4. Saute broad beans lightly in oil, then add to artichoke mixture. Add a little minced dill and cook over low heat until fully cooked. Cool. Serve.

Fresh Shelled Broad Beans with Chard and Coriander

Ingredients

1 onion

2 tablespoons ghee

1/2 kilogram meat, cubed

1 liter meat broth

Salt and pepper

1 kilogram fresh broad
beans, shelled

1 bunch each chard and
fresh coriander

4 cloves garlic

Juice of 1 lime

Method

1. Grate onion. Saute lightly in 1 tablespoon ghee until golden yellow. Add meat and stir for a few minutes. Add broth, salt, and pepper. Simmer for 30 minutes over low heat.

2. Saute broad beans lightly in 1 tablespoon ghee and add to broth mixture.

3. Wash chard and coriander leaves and pat dry. Mince with garlic, then saute lightly in ghee. Add to beans. Add lime juice and boil for 10 minutes over low heat. Serve.

Fresh Shelled Broad Beans with Meat

Ingredients

1 kilogram fresh broad
   beans, shelled
2 tablespoons ghee
2 onions
4 cloves garlic
1/2 kilogram beef, cubed
1 cup tomato juice
1 liter meat broth
Salt and pepper
1 bunch dill

Method

1. Saute broad beans lightly in 1 tablespoon ghee, preserving their green color.

2. Grate onion and saute lightly in 1 tablespoon ghee until golden yellow. Crush garlic, then add to onion. Add meat. Add tomato juice and stir for a few minutes. Add broth, salt and pepper. Cover and cook over medium heat until meat is half cooked.

3. Mince the dill. Add beans and dill to meat. Simmer over low heat until fully cooked. Serve.

Stewed Green Beans with Meat

Method

1. Prepare beans by removing stems and peeling thread-like fibers on the side, then chop them into bite-sized pieces.

2. Grate onion and season with salt and pepper. Rub onto meat.

3. Slice garlic and mix beans, onions, meat, tomato juice, broth, and ghee. Place in deep cooking pot over medium heat. Cover and cook for 30 minutes, then lower and simmer for 15 minutes until sauce thickens and ghee rises to the top. Serve.

Ingredients

1 kilogram green beans
1 onion
Salt and pepper
1/2 kilogram meat, cubed
   (beef or lamb)
2 cloves garlic
1 cup tomato juice
1 cup meat broth
2 tablespoons ghee

Stewed Zucchini with Chickpeas

Ingredients

1 kilogram large zucchini

1 onion

Salt and pepper

1/2 kilogram meat, cubed
    (beef or lamb)

1 cup tomato juice

2 cups meat broth

2 tablespoons ghee

1/4 cup small dried
    chickpeas, soaked in
    hot water for 1 hour

Method

1. Scrape zucchini skin.
   Slice zucchini into
   small rounds.

2. Grate onion and mix
   with salt and pepper.
   Rub onto meat.

3. Mix zucchini and meat.
   Add tomato juice,
   broth, ghee, and
   chickpeas.

4. Cook over medium
   heat for 30 minutes,
   then over low heat for
   15 minutes until sauce
   thickens and ghee
   rises to the top. Serve.

Zucchini and Meat Casserole

Ingredients

1 kilogram medium
  zucchini
2 tablespoons ghee
1/4 kilogram cooked
  ground beef
1/2 cup small dried
  chickpeas, soaked in
  hot water for 1 hour
1 onion
1 cup tomato juice
Salt and pepper
2 cups broth

Method

1. Cut zucchini into lengthwise pieces and fry lightly in 1 tablespoon ghee.

2. Arrange half the zucchini in an ovenproof dish. Arrange the ground beef in a layer, then add remaining zucchini. Sprinkle with chickpeas.

3. Grate onion. Saute lightly in 1 tablespoon ghee until golden yellow. Add tomato juice, salt, and pepper. Simmer until sauce thickens and ghee rises to top.

4. Add broth to tomato sauce and bring to a boil. Pour over zucchini and bake in a medium oven for 30 minutes or until sauce thickens and top is lightly browned. Serve.

Zucchini with Béchamel Sauce

Ingredients

1 kilogram medium
zucchini

Oil for deep frying

1/4 kilogram cooked
ground beef

1 egg

Butter

Béchamel sauce:

2 tablespoons flour

2 tablespoons ghee

1 cup milk

Salt and pepper

Method

1. Slice zucchini into lengthwise pieces and lightly deep fry in oil (about 5 cm deep).

2. Prepare béchamel sauce: fry flour in ghee until yellow in color, then add cold milk, salt, and pepper. Stir continuously until mixture thickens.

3. Arrange half of the fried zucchini in an ovenproof dish or Teflon baking pan. Cover with ground beef, and arrange remaining zucchini on top. Cover with béchamel sauce.

4. Beat egg with a fork. Add some pepper, brush béchamel top with egg, then add butter.

5. Bake in a medium hot oven for 30 minutes until top is lightly browned. Serve.

Cauliflower and Tomato Sauce Casserole

Ingredients

1 medium cauliflower
Salt
1 tablespoon cumin
1/4 kilogram cooked
   ground beef
2 tablespoons ghee
1 cup tomato juice
Salt and pepper
2 cups meat broth

Method

1. Separate cauliflower into medium-sized florets. Boil for 10 minutes in water to which salt and cumin have been added. Arrange in a baking pan.

2. Saute meat briefly in ghee. Add tomato juice, salt, and pepper. Cook over medium heat until sauce thickens and ghee rises to the top.

3. Add broth and bring to a boil. Pour meat and broth mixture over cauliflower. Bake in a medium hot oven for about 30 minutes or until sauce thickens and top is lightly browned. Serve.

Stewed Cauliflower with Beef

Ingredients
1 medium cauliflower
1/2 cup oil for deep frying
1 onion
2 tablespoons ghee
1/2 kilogram beef, cubed
2 cups tomato juice
Salt and pepper
1 cup meat broth

Method

1. Separate cauliflower into medium-sized florets. Deep fry in hot oil (about 5 cm deep) until just golden in color. Set aside.

2. Chop onion and saute lightly in ghee until golden yellow. Add meat and stir for a few minutes.

3. Add tomato juice, salt, and pepper. Simmer until juice thickens and ghee rises to the top.

4. Add broth and bring to a boil. Add cauliflower. Cook over medium heat for 30 minutes or until fully cooked and sauce is thickened.

Cauliflower Torte

Ingredients
1 medium cauliflower
Salt
1 tablespoon cumin
A small piece of butter
1/4 kilogram cooked ground beef
2 eggs
1/2 cup milk
2 tablespoons flour
Pepper
1 sheet waxed paper

Method

1. Separate cauliflower into medium florets. Boil for 5 minutes in salted water to which cumin has been added. Rinse with cold water.

2. Line a deep baking dish with waxed paper. Lightly grease with butter.

3. Arrange boiled cauliflower pieces in a circle. In the middle, spoon the cooked ground beef.

4. Beat the eggs, milk, flour, and pepper together. Pour over cauliflower pieces.

5. Fold waxed paper to cover top of cauliflower. Bake in a medium hot oven for 30 minutes.

6. Remove waxed paper from the top of the casserole. Turn over on a circular plate and carefully peel off the rest of the waxed paper. Serve.

Breaded Cauliflower

Ingredients

1 medium cauliflower
1 tablespoon cumin
2 tablespoons flour
2 eggs
1/2 cup milk
Salt and pepper
1 bunch parsley
Oil for deep frying

Method

1. Separate cauliflower into medium florets and soak in salted water with cumin for 5 minutes. Rinse with cold water.

2. Mix flour, eggs, milk, salt, pepper, and snipped parsley in a mixing bowl.

3. Immerse cauliflower pieces in above mixture. Coat completely. Deep fry in hot oil (about 5 cm deep) until a golden brown color. Serve hot, garnished with parsley.

Mixed Stuffed Vegetables (*Dolma*)

E gypt is well known for the quality and abundance of its fresh vegetables. Many different types of vegetables are stuffed, to be eaten as main meals for the whole family, including zucchini, eggplants, grape leaves, and cabbage leaves, while the stuffings are made of some combination of fresh herbs, tomatoes, rice, onion, ground meat, used for adding nutritious value to the meal. Stuffed vegetables are a huge favorite among Egyptians, since they contain a relatively high level of vitamins and minerals that are essential for good health, as well as rice, which is a carbohydrate, and ground meat, which is a rich source of protein.

Basic Dolma Mix

Ingredients

1 large onion
3 tablespoons each
   chopped mint and
   parsley
1/4 cup ghee
1 cup tomato juice
1 kilogram rice
   (uncooked)
1 kilogram ground beef
Salt and pepper

Method

1. Chop onion and combine with herbs.

2. Mix all ingredients well and use to stuff different vegetables.

Cooked Rice Mix

Ingredients

1 large onion
2 heaped tablespoons
   ghee
2 cups meat broth
1 cup tomato juice
Salt and pepper
1 kilogram rice
1 kilogram ground beef
3 tablespoons each
   chopped mint and
   parsley

Method

1. Chop onion and saute in ghee until golden yellow. Add broth and tomato juice. Add salt and pepper. Bring to a boil.

2. Add rice and half cook. Cool.

3. Mix ground beef, mint, and parsley with above mixture. Use to stuff desired vegetables.

Fake Dolma
(Dolma Kadhabba)

Ingredients

1 kilogram onions
1/2 liter oil
1 kilogram rice
4 cups tomato juice
1 liter broth
Salt and pepper
Juice of 10 limes
1/2 cup sugar
2 bunches parsley,
   chopped
1 bunch mint, chopped
1/4 kilogram tomatoes,
   peeled and seeded

Method

1. Finely grate onions and saute in oil. Add rice and continue stirring.

2. Add tomato juice, broth, salt, and pepper. Cook rice until almost cooked. Cool.

3. Add lime juice, sugar, parsley, mint, and tomatoes. Mix all ingredients well and use for stuffing.

Chitterlings Stuffing Mix

Ingredients
1/2 kilogram onions
1/2 kilogram tomatoes
2 tablespoons minced parsley and 1 tablespoon mint
1/2 kilogram rice
1/2 kilogram ground beef
Salt and pepper
2 tablespoons corn oil

Method

1. Grind onions with food processor and dice tomatoes.

2. Mix all ingredients well and season with salt and pepper. Add oil. Mix and use to stuff chitterlings.

Stuffed Eggplant

Ingredients
1 kilogram slender black eggplants ('arus)
1 kilogram white eggplants (abyad)
2 heaped tablespoons ghee
1/4 recipe cooked rice mix
1 tomato, sliced
1 onion, sliced
4 cloves garlic, crushed
2 tablespoons of upper part of celery stick, chopped
Bay leaf
Salt and pepper
Waxed paper
2 cups meat broth

Method

1. Core eggplants and sauté lightly in 1 tablespoon ghee.

2. Fill with cooked rice mix.

3. Line the bottom of a deep cooking pot with tomato and onion slices, crushed garlic, celery, and bay leaf. Cover with perforated waxed paper.

4. Arrange eggplants in pot in a vertical position. Season with salt and pepper. Add 1 tablespoon ghee. Cover with waxed paper, then with lid.

5. Cook for 15 minutes on top of the stove. Uncover, add broth gradually, and continue until fully cooked.

Note: Eggplants can be cooked in a Teflon pan or ovenproof baking dish. First place dish filled with eggplants in hot oven, then lower heat, adding broth gradually until fully cooked. Cover top with waxed paper before cooking.

Stuffed Chitterlings *(Mumbar mahshi)*

Method

1. Turn chitterlings inside out, using a long thin object such as a pencil or a wooden spoon handle. Rub with vinegar and salt. Scrape with a knife on both sides.

2. Turn inside out again and wash well under running water.

3. Stuff loosely with chitterling mix. Do not overstuff. Using a piece of thread, tie both ends and divide into links.

4. Boil water. Prick stuffed chitterlings to allow air to escape and drop in boiling water.

5. Add mastic grains, cardamom, and bay leaf. Boil for 1 hour. Remove from broth, cut into individual pieces, and remove thread.

6. Strain broth and add some salt.

7. Fry boiled chitterlings in ghee and serve hot with broth.

Ingredients

Ingredients
1 kilogram beef chitterlings
Vinegar
Salt
1 recipe chitterling stuffing mix
1 1/2 liters water
3–4 mastic grains
3–4 cardamom pods
Bay leaf
1 tablespoon ghee

Note: Chitterlings can be stewed in a pot in the same way as stuffed vegetables. In that case, no broth is produced.

93

Zucchini Stuffed with Ground Meat

Ingredients

1 kilogram medium or
small zucchini
1/2 kilogram tomatoes
1/2 cup boiled rice
1/4 kilogram ground beef,
cooked
Salt and pepper
1 cup tomato juice
2 tablespoons ghee

Method

1. Core zucchini and soak in salted water.

2. Immerse tomatoes in hot water for 1 minute. Rinse with cold water, peel, remove seeds, and dice.

3. Mix rice, meat, and tomatoes. Season with salt and pepper and use to stuff zucchini.

4. Arrange in a Teflon baking pan or oven-proof dish. Cover with tomato juice and ghee and bake in a medium hot oven for 30 minutes until fully cooked and sauce is thickened. Serve hot.

Meat-stuffed Potatoes and Artichokes

Ingredients

6 medium artichokes
Juice of 2 limes
1/4 cup flour
6 medium potatoes
2 tablespoons ghee
1/2 kilogram cooked
ground beef
1 onion
1 cup tomato juice
Salt and pepper
2 cups meat broth

Method

1. Prepare artichokes as previously described on page 77. Boil for 10 minutes in water to which lime juice and flour have been added.

2. Peel potatoes and core to allow for stuffing. Fry lightly in 1 table-spoon ghee.

3. Stuff artichokes and potatoes with ground beef and arrange in an oven tray.

4. Grate onion and saute lightly in 1 tablespoon ghee until golden yellow. Add tomato juice, salt, and pepper and simmer until sauce thickens and ghee rises to the top.

5. Add broth and bring to a boil. Pour over arti-chokes and potatoes. Bake in a medium hot oven for 30 minutes until fully cooked. Serve hot.

Dolma Grape leaves *(Waraq 'inab dolma)*

Ingredients

1/2 kilogram grape leaves

1/2 recipe basic dolma mix (page 91).

1 tomato, sliced

1 onion, sliced

4 cloves garlic, crushed

3–4 sticks celery

Bay leaf

2 tablespoons ghee

Juice of 2 limes

Salt and pepper

2 cups meat broth

Method

1. Remove stems from grape leaves. Boil in salted water for 5 minutes. Rinse with cold water.

2. Spread out individual leaves. Place a small amount of the filling at the base of each leaf. Fold edges while rolling tightly. Continue stuffing leaves doing so until you run out of filling.

3. In the bottom of a deep pot arrange in layers the tomato and half the onion slices, crushed garlic, celery, bay leaf, and some of the grape leaves left over from stuffing.

4. Arrange stuffed grape leaves in layers. Add ghee, lime juice, salt, pepper, and the broth. Cover with the rest of the onion slices and cook for 30 minutes. Serve hot.

Grape Leaves with Shanks

Ingredients
1/2 kilogram grape leaves
1/2 recipe basic dolma mix (page 91).
1 veal shank
1 tomato, sliced
1 onion, sliced
4 cloves garlic, crushed
Celery
Bay leaf
2 tablespoons ghee
Salt and pepper
Juice of 1 lime
2 cups broth

Method

1. Prepare grape leaves and stuff as described opposite.

2. Boil shanks for two hours then remove bone.

3. In a deep cooking pot, arrange layers of tomato and onion slices, garlic, celery, bay leaf, and leftover grape leaves. Place shanks on top. Arrange stuffed grape leaves in layers.

4. Add ghee, salt, pepper, lime juice, and broth. Cook for 30 minutes. Add broth gradually while continuing to cook until well done.

5. Invert onto a large serving plate. Remove the tomato and onion slices and the unstuffed grape leaves. Serve hot.

Stuffed Cabbage Leaves

Ingredients
1 medium cabbage
1/2 recipe basic dolma mix, (page 91) with 2 tablespoons chopped dill
2 tablespoons ghee
Salt and pepper
2 cups meat broth

Method

1. Separate cabbage leaves from the base using the tip of a knife. Remove stem. Cut leaves horizontally into three parts.

2. Heat a pot of water and add salt. Immerse leaves in hot water until softened and wilted (about 2 minutes). Rinse with cold water. Do not boil.

3. Prepare dolma mix. Stuff and roll individual cabbage pieces. Use a knife to trim edges.

4. Arrange some of the leftover cabbage leaves in a deep pot, then add stuffed cabbage leaves. Add ghee, salt, pepper, and broth.

5. Cook for 30 minutes. Serve hot.

Stuffed Lettuce Leaves

Same ingredients and steps as for Stuffed Cabbage Leaves (page 97), but substitute lettuce leaves.

Mixed Stuffed Vegetables with Meat
(Dolma mishakila bi-l-lahm)

Ingredients
1/2 kilogram medium or small zucchini
1/2 kilogram small sweet peppers
1/2 kilogram round tomatoes, of uniform size
Salt and pepper
1/2 recipe cooked rice mix
1 tomato, sliced
1 onion, sliced
2 sticks celery, sliced into pieces
2 tablespoons of upper part of celery stick, chopped
Bay leaf
4 cloves garlic, crushed
2 tablespoons ghee
1 tablespoon lime juice
2 cups meat broth
Waxed paper

Method

1. Core zucchini and soak in salted water.

2. Slice pepper caps horizontally and remove seeds. Retain caps and stems to use as covers after stuffing.

3. Slice through the upper part of the tomatoes horizontally to remove caps. Using a spoon, core tomatoes. Season insides with salt and pepper, invert, and set aside for 5 minutes. Stuff vegetables with cooked rice mix. Or, you may use the basic dolma mix.

4. Arrange tomato and onion slices, celery, bay leaf, and crushed garlic in the bottom of the deep pot. Cover with perforated waxed paper. Arrange stuffed vegetables vertically.

5. Add ghee, lime juice, salt, and pepper. Cover with waxed paper, then with pot lid. Cook for 15 minutes, then uncover, and start adding broth gradually until fully stewed. Serve hot.

Dolma with Oil

Prepare in the same way as previous recipe but use the fake dolma mix instead of the cooked rice mix. Add extra lime juice and serve cold. All types of vegetables can be prepared in this way.

Meats

P roteins are the most important building block for animal cells as they are the only macronutrient from which tissue building and repair can occur. Proteins are made up of individual building units known as amino acids.

There are 20 known amino acids; they are found in proteins containing foods in the form of chains of different amino acid combinations. Protein digestion is the breakdown of these chains into individual amino acids to allow their absorption. They are then carried by the blood to the various parts of the body for use.

Different tissues in the body utilize amino acids to maintain their structures. As many of the foods we eat do not contain all of the amino acids, a variety of vegetable and animal protein sources is recommended to ensure meeting the body's requirements.

Protein Sources

A: Animal sources such as meat, poultry, fish, eggs, and milk products.

B: Plant sources such as grains and legumes.

We must be familiar with the characteristics of the different meats available in the market so as to be able to identify them and make use of them in the best way.

Lamb *(Dani)* is one of the most preferred by Egyptians in spite of its high fat content and low nutritional value. Good cuts of meat come from lambs 9–24 months old.

Meat that comes from an animal slaughtered before its first year of life is light pink in color. The color gets darker as an animal ages, turning red in older animals.

As a general rule, the younger the lamb the better the meat. The best meat comes from lambs less than 6 months old, when the meat is light pink and the fat is yellowish white. A light blue color of the ribs and joints indicates young age in an animal. A usual serving size for an adult is 250 grams with bones and 175 grams without.

Calf (Veal) *(Bitillu)* is easy to digest but of low nutritional value. Veal comes from calves slaughtered between the second and third month of age. The meat is usually a light red color, delicate and free of thick membranes and dense fat. Although veal is a type of beef, it has completely different characteristics. The best meat comes from animals that have been slaughtered before weaning, whose only food had been milk. Generally veal is low in fat so it is used in dishes requiring cooking over low heat. The adult serving size is 250 grams with bones and 175 grams without.

Cow (Beef) *(Sambari* **or** *Canduz)* is one of the best types of meat due to its high nutritional value. The color of the meat is bright red and it is permeated by fat that has a yellowish tinge. Many delicious dishes can be prepared from some of the cheaper beef cuts, although they may require prolonged cooking (around three hours). Cuts covered with a thin layer of fat or streaked with fat are considered to be the best cuts because of their rich flavor and in spite of their high fat content. One can remove the excess fat before use. Generally, the parts closest to the bone are the tastiest. The adult serving size for beef is 250 grams with bones and 125 grams without.

Camel *(Gamali)* meat is one of the most popular meats among Egyptians, who have known it since ancient times. Because camel meat is so favored, Egyptians had special markets for camels and special routes known as "camel paths" along which merchants traveled when bringing the animals from Sudan to Egypt. Camel meat has a special flavor, close to that of beef. The meat is bright red in color and the fat located in the hump is translucent.

Camels normally live around twenty five years, reaching maturity at the age of sixteen. Camels are slaughtered for meat between the ages of two and four years. After that age the meat would be too tough to cook or eat. Even so, camel meat takes a long time to cook, between three and four hours when cooked in liquid. One of the dishes commonly prepared from camel meat is rice kufta, as it holds its shape well with prolonged cooking.

Camel broth is transparent and contains no fat. Therefore, a piece of hump fat is added along with tomato juice to give taste and color. Usually "*marta*" mix is used to season camel meat before boiling. The *marta* mix is a grated onion seasoned with salt, pepper, and cumin. This mixture is rubbed onto the camel meat, which is cooked over medium low heat until all juices are absorbed into the meat. Extra liquid is then added and it is boiled until fully cooked.

Rules that Must be Followed when Buying Meat

Make sure that the meat is fresh, young, and has a pleasant odor. Beef must be bright red, lamb and veal must be pink. The color of fat must be pale yellow.

There should be no blue spots near the bone and fatty areas. Marrow must be firm and reddish in color.

Meat must have the slaughterhouse stamp of approval that indicates that it is free from diseases.

A red rectangular stamp indicates that the animal is young in age, while a red triangular stamp indicates that the animal is older than four years. A purple stamp indicates that the animal is imported but has been slaughtered locally.

On applying pressure with fingers, no indentations should be left on the meat. The inside membranes must be thin, clear, and complete.

When buying ground meat, look for a bright red, not grayish, color. It is preferable to buy a whole piece of meat and have it freshly ground with the addition of a piece of beef or lamb fat to give extra flavor.

Use ground beef right away, or store it in the freezer just after grinding, as it is more likely to harbor the growth of bacteria than whole cuts.

Advice for the Preparation of Different Meat Dishes

Ground beef is used in the preparation of many dishes, such as grilled or fried kuftas, macaroni with béchamel and pasta sauce, vegetable stuffing mixes and dulmas. Ground beef is also used to prepare sausage links or *suguq*, meat-filled bread, and different types of pies.

When grilling meats, it is preferable to use prime cuts of tenderloin, steak, or lamb chops, making sure to marinate them for at least 1 hour before grilling.

Meat must be brought to room temperature before grilling over medium heat.

Grilling time should not be prolonged. Grilling over coals or wood is one of the best ways, as it gives meat a good flavor.

When using a double grill or a Teflon pan, the grill must be well heated and the meat must be coated with a layer of oil or butter. Do not use a fork for turning meat over, as punctures drain the meat juices away. If making veal Kebabs, meat must be cut into small cubes, seasoned with herbs, spices, yogurt, and garlic and left to marinate for at least two hours before grilling.

If making breaded fried meat, it is better to use thin slices from the top of the leg or thin slices of tenderloin. Meat must be pounded until thin, then seasoned with salt, pepper, and onion juice, covered with egg, then coated with a layer of fine dried breadcrumbs and deep fried in hot ghee.

There are two techniques for frying:

Rapid frying in ghee: Heat two tablespoons of ghee, then add pieces of meat, whole onion, garlic cloves, and black pepper while stirring constantly until meat is browned on all sides. Then add water gradually until meat is fully cooked; then add salt. This technique has the advantage of being fast while allowing meat to retain its color and tenderness.

Slow frying: This requires only about 1 tablespoon of ghee. Cook meat slices on medium high heat for a few minutes on each side until they acquire a brown color. Then reduce the heat and gradually add the broth; leave the meat to simmer, covered. This method takes longer and might result in somewhat drier meat.

There are two ways to boil meat:

Boiling in hot water: water is brought to a boil, then meat, onion, seasonings, and vegetables are added. This method allows the meat to retain its juices and nutrients.

Boiling in cold water: meat is rinsed and covered with cold water, then brought to a boil. Froth is removed then onion, seasonings, and vegetables are added. This methods allow for a richer soup.

Note It is generally preferred to add salt to meat after it is fully cooked as salt delays cooking.

Leg of Lamb with Potatoes
(Serves 10, cooking time approximately 3 hours)

Method

1. Wash leg well, remove stamp and the thick outer membranes. Break the thigh bone *(femur)* and place in an oven pan.

2. Season well with salt and pepper. Using the tip of a knife, make several small cuts around the leg and fill them with whole garlic cloves and pepper-corns.

3. Melt ghee and pour over meat. Bake in a medium hot oven, basting occasionally until half cooked.

4. Prepare poatoes by peeling, cubing, and boiling in water for a few minutes. Arrange around leg of the lamb. Season with salt, pepper, bay leaf, and garlic. Cover and continue baking, basting occaionally until fully cooked.

5. Cool meat enough to handle, then carve into even slices. Place in a serving dish and arrange cooked pota-toes in circles around the meat.

6. Mix broth with the drippings that remain in the oven pan. Boil, strain, then pour over lamb and potatoes. Serve hot.

Ingredients

Ingredients
1 small leg of lamb (about 2 1/2 kilograms)
Salt and pepper
10 garlic cloves
1 teaspoon peppercorns
2 heaped tablespoons ghee
Bay leaf
1 kilogram potatoes
1 cup broth

Leg of Lamb with Mixed Vegetables
(Serves 10, cooking time approximately 3 hours)

Ingredients

1 small leg of lamb
Salt and pepper
Bay leaf
5 cups broth
1/4 kilogram pearl onions
2 cloves garlic
2 heaped tablespoons
 ghee
1 teaspoon sugar
1/4 kilogram carrots
1 tablespoon butter
1/4 kilogram potatoes
1/4 kilogram green peas

Method

1. Wash leg of lamb, break thigh bone, season well with salt and pepper, and place in an oven pan. Add bay leaf, 2 cups broth, 2 onions, 2 cloves garlic, and melted ghee. Cover and place in a medium hot oven, basting frequently with drippings until well done.

2. Peel remaining pearl onions and lightly fry them in 1 tablespoon ghee. Add 1 cup broth, salt, and 1/2 teaspoon sugar. Cover and simmer until fully cooked.

3. Peel carrots. Cut into short sticks and boil for 5 minutes. Drain and place in a saucepan. Add 1 tablespoon butter, salt, 1/2 teaspoon sugar, and 1 cup broth. Cover and simmer until well done.

4. Peel and cut potatoes as carrots. Boil in water, drain, and fry in ghee.

5. Shell peas and saute in butter over low heat for 30 minutes.

6. When meat is cool enough to handle, cut it into slices and arrange them in a serving dish surrounded by the cooked vegetables.

7. Mix 1 cup broth with drippings in pan. Boil for 5 minutes then strain. Pour some sauce over the leg of lamb. Serve the rest of the sauce in a separate bowl beside the lamb and vegetables dish. The consistency of the sauce should be thick.

Leg of Lamb with Islambuli Rice

Ingredients

Leg of lamb:

1 small leg of lamb
Salt and pepper
Bay leaf
1 cup broth
2 onions
2 cloves garlic
2 heaped tablespoons
    ghee
1 recipe rice red base

Islambuli rice:

1 kilogram rice
1 liter water for
    soaking rice
1 teaspoon salt
1 cup ghee
1 1/2 cups peeled
    almonds
1 1/2 cups pine nuts
1 1/2 cups shelled
    pistachios
1/2 cup raisins
2 liters red base for rice
    (see recipe opposite)
1/4 kilogram chicken
    livers
Salt and pepper

Method for lamb

1. Prepare and cook leg of lamb as in step 1 of previous recipe (see page 107).

2. Prepare Islambuli rice and place in a large serving dish.

3. Slice leg of lamb evenly and arrange slices over rice.

4. Add broth to remaining dippings. Boil and strain. Pour some of the sauce over the lamb and serve the rest in separate bowl.

Method for rice

1. Soak rice in hot salted water for 1 hour.

2. Heat ghee. Add almonds and fry lightly, then add pine nuts, then pistachios, and finally raisins, lightly frying all while stirring for a few minutes. Remove from ghee. Drain nuts and raisins on paper towels.

3. Drain rice and sauté it in ghee over medium low heat, stirring constantly until rice grains become golden. Strain from ghee.

4. Sauté chicken livers in ghee for 5 minutes and season them with salt and pepper.

5. Boil red rice base, then add rice, fried nuts, and chicken livers to it. Cover and cook over low heat for 15 minutes. Remove from heat.

Red base for rice:

1 kilogram lamb or veal
   bones
1/2 cup ghee
1 large onion
2 stalks each leeks and
   celery
1/2 kilogram tomatoes,
   halved and seeded
3 liters water or broth
Salt and pepper
2 cardamom pods

Method for red base for rice

1. Wash bones and pat dry. Heat ghee, adds bones, and sauté

2. Mince onion, leeks, and celery. Add to bones, stirring constantly until vegetables are golden brown. Add tomatoes and stir with bones until all liquid is absorbed

3. Add broth or water along with salt, pepper, and cardamom. Remove froth as it forms. Cover and simmer for 2 hours until fully cooked

4. Strain in a colander, then again through a cheesecloth-lined colander. Use to make islambuli rice (opposite).

Side of Lamb with Islambuli Rice

Ingredients

Side of a small lamb
Salt and pepper
2 heaped tablespoons
   ghee
2 onions, whole
Bay leaf
1 cup broth
1 recipe Islambuli Rice
   (see page 108).

Method

1. Prepare side of lamb. Remove kidneys and excess fat. Peel outside membrane by holding it from the top and pulling it away all the way to the end. Use string to hold the bones together. Season with salt and pepper and place in an oven pan.

2. Heat ghee and sprinkle over lamb. Add onions and bay leaf. Cook in a medium hot oven, basting occasionally with drippings, for 3 hours or until done.

3. Remove meat and boil broth with drippings in oven pan for about 5 minutes until the mixture has a sauce-like constituency. Strain.

4. Untie string. Remove the lamb with a knife. Slice the roast, then return it to its cavity.

5. Prepare Islambuli rice. Arrange in a rectangular dish and place lamb on top. Sprinkle with a little sauce and serve remaining sauce in a side dish.

Side of Lamb, Egyptian Style

Same as previous recipe, but serve surrounded by mixed dolma, such as tomatoes, zucchini, grape leaves, and sweet peppers, stuffed with meat (see recipes on pages 91–92).

Lamb Rib Roast

(Serves 4, cooking time approx. 2 hours)

Prepared in the same way as side of lamb with Islambuli rice.

Paper-wrapped Meat Baked in the Oven

Ingredients
1 kilogram rib chops
1/2 kilogram boneless rib roast
1/4 kilogram lamb liver
1/4 kilogram kidneys
Salt and pepper
1/4 teaspoon nutmeg
1/2 kilogram onions
Aluminum foil

Method

1. Prepare rib chops and boneless rib roast, cube liver, and cut kidneys in slices. Season with salt, pepper, and ground nutmeg.

2. Slice onions and mix with all the ingredients. Wrap meats in aluminum foil.

3. Bake in a hot oven for at least an hour. Remove meats from foil, place in a round dish, and serve.

Roast Beef (*'Irq al-lahm al-barid*)

Ingredients

1 medium pot roast
(about 2 kilograms)
Salt and pepper
1/2 teaspoon
peppercorns
6 cloves garlic, whole
2 tablespoons ghee
Bay leaf
1 cup broth

Method

1. Wash roast and pat dry. Tie up with string to maintain shape while cooking.

2. Season with salt and pepper. Cut slits with the tip of a knife and stuff them with pepper-corns and garlic cloves. Place roast in a cooking pan.

3. Melt ghee and use to coat the roast. Saute, turning occasionally until it is browned on all sides. Add bay leaf. Cover and bake in a medium hot oven, basting from time to time, for two hours or until fully cooked. If necessary, you may add a little broth during cooking to prevent

the meat from drying. Remove roast from pan.

4. Add broth to meat drippings. Boil, then strain. The sauce should be thick.

5. Allow the roast to cool completely, then cut into thin slices using a sharp knife. Arrange in a serving dish with sauce, heated, on the side.

Goat's Meat
(Nifa)

Ingredients
Lamb or goat ribs, 1 piece (1 1/2 to 2 kilograms)
Salt and pepper
2 tablespoons ghee
Bay leaf

Method

1. Prepare meat by sawing through bones and peeling the thin skin that covers the meat. With a knife, make incomplete cuts between each rib. The ribs should be kept in one piece.

2. Season with salt and pepper and place in an oven tray. Melt ghee and coat ribs. Add bay leaf and cover. Place in a medium hot oven for 1 hour, stirring occasionally, until fully cooked and browned on both sides.

3. Separate ribs and serve.

Shish Kebab

Ingredients

1 kilogram lamb or beef,
    cubed
Salt and pepper
1 tablespoon thyme
Bay leaf
1 tablespoon lime juice
1 cup yogurt
1 tablespoon corn oil
Parsley for garnish
Onion, tomato, and
    sweet pepper cubes,
    optional

Method

1. Combine salt, pepper, thyme, bay leaf, lime juice, yogurt, and oil, and add to meat cubes. Marinate for at least 30 minutes.

2. Thread meat cubes on skewers and grill on both sides on a double grill for about 10 minutes a side. Serve on a bed of parsley.

Note: You may add onion, tomato, and sweet pepper cubes, threading them alternately with meat cubes on the skewers.

113

Coal-grilled Mixed Kebab

Ingredients
1 kilogram veal (chops or round)
1/2 kilogram liver
1/2 kilogram kidneys
2 beef testicles
Salt and pepper
Bay leaf
1 large grated onion, pressed through a sieve
1/2 cup oil
1 small cup yogurt
1 tablespoon thyme
Parsley stems for basting
Parsley sprigs for garnishing

Method

1. Cube veal, liver, and kidneys.

2. Peel outside membranes from testicles and cut into quarters.

3. Combine salt, pepper, bay leaf, onion juice, oil, yogurt, and thyme, and add to meat. Marinate for 30 minutes.

4. Prepare Kebabs by alternating cubes of meat and organs on the skewers. Grill on coals for 10 minutes, turning skewers on all sides and basting frequently with marinade using a brush or parsley stems.

5. Remove Kebabs from skewers and place on a dish, garnished with parsley. Serve.

Pot Kebab (Kabab halla)

Ingredients
1 kilogram veal or beef, cubed
1 onion
2 cloves garlic, whole
2 cups broth
Salt and pepper
2 tablespoons ghee

Method

1. Heat ghee. Add meat, onion, and garlic. Stir for a few minutes.

2. Cover pot and allow meat juices to be absorbed and meat to brown. Add broth gradually. Add pepper.

3. Before meat is cooked, add salt, and stir meat cubes in ghee until there is a thick brown sauce. Serve.

Meat Casserole with Chickpeas *(Yakhni)*

Ingredients

1 kilogram meat (round
   or shin)
1/2 kilogram onions
6 cloves garlic
2 tablespoons ghee
1/2 cup chickpeas
2 cups tomato juice
Salt and pepper
1 tablespoon mixed spice
2 cups water or broth

Method

1. Cut meat into small cubes. Slice onions and garlic.

2. Heat ghee. Fry onions, then garlic, until golden yellow. Add meat cubes and stir for a few minutes. Add chickpeas. Stir ingredients for a few minutes.

3. Add tomato juice, pepper, and buharat. Cook until sauce is thickened and ghee rises to the top. Add broth or water and cook over low heat.

4. Transfer ingredients into an earthenware container (bram) and bake in a medium hot oven until fully cooked, about 15 minutes. Add salt and serve.

Meat in Tomato Sauce

Ingredients

1 onion
4 cloves garlic
2 tablespoon ghee
1 kilogram shin meat, cubed
4 cups water or broth
2 cups tomato juice
Salt and pepper

Method

1. Peel onion and garlic. Saute lightly whole in ghee until golden yellow. Add meat and saute until browned. Add half the broth and simmer until fully cooked.

2. Add tomato juice and pepper. Cook until sauce thickens and ghee rises to the top.

3. Add the remaining broth and cook over low heat until boiling. Add salt and serve.

Breaded Fried Liver

(Kibda panée)

Ingredients

1/2 kilogram veal liver
Salt and pepper
1 teaspoon lime juice
1/2 cup flour
Corn oil or ghee for deep frying

Method

1. Remove membranes and blood vessels from liver. Slice horizontally into 1/2 cm thick slices. Season with salt and pepper, and lime juice. Coat with flour and fry in oil or ghee on both sides until browned.

2. Arrange on a plate and serve.

Fried Liver

Ingredients

1/2 kilogram veal or lamb liver
Salt and pepper
2 cloves garlic, sliced
2 tablespoons ghee

Method

1. Prepare liver as described in previous recipe. Season with salt, pepper, and garlic.

2. Heat ghee. Fry liver for 10 minutes, stirring continuously. Serve.

Grilled Liver

Ingredients
1/2 kilogram veal or lamb liver
Salt and pepper
1 tablespoon thyme
1 tablespoon oil
1 tablespoon lime juice

Method

1. Prepare liver as described on page 117. Season with salt, pepper, thyme, and oil. Marinate for 30 minutes, then grill, using a double grill or Teflon pan.

2. Arrange on a plate. Squeeze lime juice on liver and serve.

Liver with Cumin Seasoning

Ingredients
1/2 kilogram beef liver
1 onion
2 tablespoons ghee or corn oil
4 cloves garlic, crushed
1 cup tomato juice
Salt and pepper
1 tablespoon cumin

Method

1. Peel thin membranes covering liver. Remove blood vessels. Cut into medium-sized cubes.

2. Grate onion and saute lightly in ghee or oil. Add liver cubes and stir for a few minutes. Add garlic and continue stirring until liver is lightly browned.

3. Add tomato juice, salt, pepper, and cumin. Continue cooking until sauce thickens and ghee rises to top. Serve.

Alexandria Style Liver

Ingredients

1/2 kilogram beef liver
5 cloves garlic
1 hot chili pepper
1 tablespoon dried
    coriander
1 tablespoon cumin
Salt and pepper
Juice of 2 limes
1/2 cup corn oil

Method

1. Remove outside membranes covering liver. Remove blood vessels. Chop into small, thin pieces. Wash, then drain in a colander.

2. Crush garlic, chili, coriander, cumin, salt, and pepper. Add to liver along with half of the lime juice. Marinate for 30 minutes.

3. Heat oil. Add liver pieces gradually, stirring constantly. (The oil must be kept hot at all times, which is why the liver must be added gradually.)

4. When liver is half cooked (after about 5 minutes), lower heat, cover and cook for 10 minutes.

5. Remove lid, raise heat, and stir continuously until liver pieces are lightly browned. Season with the remaining lime juice and serve.

Fried Testicles *(Makhassi mihamara)*

Ingredients
2 beef testicles
Salt and pepper
2 tablespoons ghee

Method

1. Remove outside membrane covering testicles. Cut into 4 pieces. Place in a skillet.

2. Season with salt and pepper. Add ghee and cook over low heat for about 10 minutes until liquid is absorbed.

3. Saute until lightly browned. Serve

Spleen *(Tuhal)*

Ingredients
1 liter water
Salt and pepper
1 beef spleen
2 tablespoons ghee
1 teaspoon lime juice

Method

1. Add salt and pepper to water and bring to a boil. Add spleen and cook for 15 minutes.

2. Remove from water and cool. Remove outside membrane, and season spleen with salt and pepper.

Coat with ghee, place in an ovenproof dish and cook in a medium hot oven for 10 minutes. Remove from oven.

3. Cut into thin slices. Pour lime juice over slices and serve.

Tongue *(Lisan)*

Ingredients

1 liter water

1 beef tongue

1 onion

3–4 mastic grains

3–4 cardamom pods

Bay leaf

Salt and pepper

1 tablespoon ghee

Method

1. Boil water. Wash tongue, then place in boiling water. Remove froth as it forms.

2. Add onion, mastic grains, cardamom, bay leaf, and pepper. Cook tongue in boiling water for 30 minutes. Poke a sharp knife all the way through in several places to ensure complete cooking. Add salt 5 minutes before tongue is completely cooked.

3. Remove tongue from liquid. Place in an oven tray and season with salt and pepper. Coat with ghee and place in a medium hot oven for 10 minutes or until lightly browned. Cool.

4. Using a sharp knife, remove outside membrane. Cool in refrigerator, then cut into thin slices and serve cold.

Boiled Brain

Ingredients

1/2 liter water

Salt and pepper

1 beef brain

1 tablespoon lime juice

1 tablespoon chopped
parsley

Method

1. Boil water. Add salt
   and pepper.

2. Wash brain. Place in
   boiling water and boil
   for 10 minutes.

3. Drain water and allow
   brain to cool. Peel off
   outside membrane and
   blood vessels.

4. Slice and season with
   salt, pepper, and lime.
   Garnish with parsley
   and serve cold.

Breaded Fried Brain

Ingredients

Ingredients
1/2 liter water
1 beef brain
1 egg
Salt and pepper
1/2 cup flour
2 tablespoons ghee or oil for frying
Parsley sprigs for garnish

Method

1. Clean, boil, and slice brain as previously described (see page 122).

2. Beat egg with fork and season with salt and pepper. Coat brain slices with egg.

3. Coat brain slices well with flour. Fry in ghee or oil until golden brown. Serve on plate, garnished with parsley.

Baked Head of Lamb

Method

1. Clean the head from the outside. Split in two, keeping the brain inside. This is a difficult task to do at home, so it is advisable to ask a butcher to do it.

2. Boil water. Add onion and head of lamb. Bring to a boil, removing any froth that forms.

3. Add pepper, mastic, cardamom, and bay leaf. Cook over medium heat for 1 hour until fully cooked.

Ingredients

Ingredients
1 lamb head
1 1/2 liters water
1 onion
Salt and pepper
3–4 mastic grains
3–4 cardamom pods
Bay leaf
2 tablespoons ghee

4. Remove head from liquid and season with salt and pepper. Coat in ghee and bake in a medium hot oven for 30 minutes until lightly browned.

5. To serve, separate the meat from the bone and remove the brain from within the skull to be served on the side. Serve hot, or refrigerate and serve cold.

Fried Lamb Organs

Ingredients

1 liter water

Lamb throat, lungs, liver,
and heart (organs)

Salt and pepper

4 cloves garlic, sliced

2 tablespoons ghee

Method

1. Boil water and season with salt and pepper. Add throat and lungs and boil for 30 minutes. Strain and cool.

2. Cube liver and heart. Season with salt, pepper, and garlic. In a skillet, place cubed organs and ghee and cook over medium heat for a few minutes, stirring occasionally.

3. Cube throat and lungs. Add to other ingredients. Continue cooking over medium heat, stirring occasionally until liquid is absorbed and top is lightly browned. Serve.

Sweetbreads Casserole *(Tagin halawiyat)*

Ingredients
1 onion
4 cloves garlic
Salt and pepper
1/2 kilogram veal or beef sweetbreads (thyroid gland)
2 cups tomato juice
1 tablespoon corn oil, if needed

Method

1. Slice onion and garlic. Season with salt and pepper.

2. Chop sweetbreads into small pieces. Combine with onion. Add tomato juice and oil if needed. Sweetbreads are very high in fat, so oil may be unnecessary, depending on the amount of fat generated during cooking; however beef is leaner than veal, so may need additional oil.

3. Bring mixture to a boil, then cook over medium heat for 15 minutes. Pour into an ovenproof dish and bake in a medium hot oven for 30 minutes until sauce thickens and fat rises to the top. Serve hot. (Do not serve cold, as a layer of fat will form on the top.)

Sweetbreads with Green Mallow
(Halawiyat bi-l-mulukhiyya)

Method

1. Boil water. Chop onion, and season with salt and pepper. Add to water, and boil for a few minutes. Add sweetbreads and cook over medium heat for 15 minutes.

2. Finely chop fresh green mallow or dried green mallow. Add to sweetbreads. Cook for 2 minutes, stirring constantly, then remove from heat.

3. Crush garlic and dried coriander. Fry in ghee and pour on top of dish. Serve hot.

Ingredients
1 liter water
1 onion
Salt and pepper
1/2 kilogram veal sweetbreads (thyroid glands), chopped
1 kilogram fresh green mallow or 1 cup dried green mallow
4 cloves garlic
2 tablespoons dried coriander
1 tablespoon ghee

Tripe Casserole with Chickpeas

Ingredients

1 kilogram boiled tripe
(see recipe for Boiled
Tripe Soup on page 36)
2 large onions
5 cloves garlic
Salt and pepper
1 cup tomato juice
1 cup water
2 tablespoons ghee
1/2 cup small dried chickpeas, soaked in hot
water for 1 hour

Method

1. Chop boiled tripe into small pieces and place in an ovenproof dish or *bram.*

2. Slice onions and garlic. Season with salt and pepper and add to tripe. Add tomato juice, water, and ghee.

3. Add chickpeas. Cook over medium heat for 30 minutes. Place in an earthenware dish *(bram).*

4. Bake in a medium hot oven for 15 minutes until fully cooked and with a thick sauce. Serve.

Coccyx and Tail Casserole
(Tagin 'akawi wi halalat)

Ingredients

1 kilogram beef coccyx
and tail
1 cup tomato juice
1 cup water
Salt and pepper
1/4 teaspoon nutmeg
2 tablespoons ghee
1/2 kilogram onions, sliced
5 cloves garlic, sliced

Method

1. Chop coccyx and tail and soak in water for 15 minutes. Drain and place in a cooking pot.

2. Add tomato juice, water, salt, pepper, and nutmeg. Add ghee, onions, and garlic.

3. Cook over medium heat for at least 1 hour. Transfer to an oven-proof baking dish and bake in a medium hot oven for 15 minutes until sauce thickens and ghee rises to the top. Serve hot.

Head Meat Casserole with Chickpeas

Ingredients

1 kilogram head meat
  (beef or veal)
1/4 kilogram veal sweet-
  breads, optional
1/2 kilogram onions
Salt and pepper
5 cloves garlic
Mixed spice
1 cup tomato juice
1 cup water
2 tablespoons ghee
1/2 cup small dried chi
  peas, soaked in hot
  water for 1 hour

Method

1. Chop head meat into small pieces. You may add some chopped veal sweetbreads (thyroid gland), if desired.

2. Slice onions and season with salt and pepper. Slice garlic and combine with mixed spice. Mix all of this with meat.

3. Add tomato juice, water, ghee (if adding thyroid gland, omit ghee), and chickpeas.

4. Cook over medium heat for 30 minutes. Transfer to an oven-proof dish and bake until sauce is thickened and top is lightly browned. Serve.

127

Shank and Chickpea Casserole

Ingredients

2 beef shanks
2 onions
Salt and pepper
5 cloves garlic
1/4 teaspoon nutmeg
1 cup tomato juice
1 cup water
2 tablespoons ghee
1/2 cup small dried
chickpeas, soaked in
hot water for 1 hour

Method

1. Boil shanks until almost cooked. Remove bones and cut meat into small pieces. (see page 35).

2. Prepare in the same way as previous recipe (page 127) substituting the nutmeg for the mixed spice. Serve hot.

Coal-grilled Kufta

Ingredients

1 onion
1 kilogram ground beef
1/4 kilogram ground lamb
Salt and pepper
1/2 teaspoon mixed spice
1/4 cup corn oil
1 tablespoon chopped
parsley

Method

1. Grate the onion and squeeze out its juice. Mix onion, ground meats, salt, pepper, and mixed spice, blending thoroughly. Set aside for at least 1 hour to allow the flavors to develop.

2. Shape individual kuftas around metal skewers, pressing firmly to make them finger-shaped. Grill over hot coals, brushing occasionally with oil until completely done. Serve hot, garnished with parsley.

3. For indoor grilling, use either a double grill on the stove top or a Teflon skillet. Grill kufta, then place in a metal or ceramic container and cover. Heat a piece of coal until red hot and place in the center of the container, pushing the kufta to the side. Spoon some oil onto the hot coal to produce smoke and keep covered 5 minutes. Serve hot, garnished with parsley.

Oven-grilled Kufta

Method

1. Prepare kufta mixture but do not shape on skewers. Shape individual kuftas and arrange them in a pan. Cover with tomato and sweet pepper slices. Sprinkle with salt and pepper.

2. Drizzle kufta with melted ghee. Add water and bake in medium hot oven for about 30 minutes or until kufta is well done and tops are browned. Serve hot.

Kufta Wrapped in Omentum
(Kufta bi-l-tarab)

Ingredients

Ingredients
1 onion
1 kilogram ground beef
Salt and pepper
1/2 teaspoon mixed spice
Lamb omentum *(tarab)* (the outer sac of the intenstine)
1/2 cup water
Chopped parsley

Method

1. Prepare kufta in the same way as for Coal-grilled Kufta (page 128).

2. Cut omentum into small rectangles. Wrap individual kuftas in pieces of cut omentum. Arrange in an oven tray and season with salt and pepper.

3. Pour water in tray and bake in a medium hot oven for 30 minutes until fully cooked. Serve, garnished with chopped parsley.

Rice Kufta

Ingredients

1/2 kilogram ground beef
1 small onion, grated
2 cloves garlic
1 tablespoon each
   chopped mint and
   parsley
1 cup rice
Salt and pepper
1 teaspoon mixed spice
Oil for deep frying

Method

1. Mix beef, grated onion, garlic, mint, and parsley.

2. Soak rice in water for 15 minutes. Drain, grind, then add to meat mixture. Add salt, pepper, and spices.

3. Mix all ingredients well, then blend in a food processor until smooth and thoroughly combined.

4. Grease palm of hand lightly. Shape kufta into small balls or fingers and deep fry in hot oil (about 5 cm deep).

Note: 1. Ground camel meat can be used instead of beef, as it holds its shape well.
2. Fine bulgur can be used instead of rice for a softer kufta. Soak bulgur for 30 minutes, squeeze water out as much as possible, then grind. Use 1/4 kilogram ground bulgur for each kilogram meat.

Rice Kufta with Tomato Sauce and Potato Wedges

Ingredients

1 kilogram fried rice kufta (page 132)

1/2 kilogram potatoes, sliced into wedges

4 tablespoons corn oil

1 small onion

2 cloves garlic

4 mastic grains

Salt and pepper

1 cup tomato juice

1 liter meat broth

Method

1. Prepare kufta as described in previous recipe. Fry potato wedges in oil until half cooked.

2. Heat oil. Fry whole onion until golden yellow. Add garlic cloves and fry until golden yellow. Add mastic grains and pepper. Add tomato juice and cook until sauce thickens.

3. Add broth and a little salt. Bring to a boil, then add kufta and fried potatoes. Cook over medium heat for 15 minutes, then lower heat and simmer for 10 minutes until sauce thickens.

Note: Rice kufta with tomato sauce can be served alongside couscous as a savory dish.

133

Kufta Roll with Eggs

Ingredients

1/2 baguette loaf
1/2 cup milk
1 kilogram lean ground
   beef
Salt and pepper
1/2 teaspoon mixed spice
1 onion, grated
1 tablespoon chopped
   parsley
4 eggs
Sheep omentum or sheet
   of waxed paper
1/2 cup water
1 tablespoon ghee

Method

1. Soak bread in milk for 15 minutes.

2. Season meat with salt, pepper, and mixed spice. Add grated onion and chopped parsley.

3. Remove bread from milk, squeeze out any extra liquid and add to meat. Beat 1 egg with a fork and add. Mix all ingredients well.

4. Hardboil remaining 3 eggs. Cool, and remove shells.

5. Spread out omentum or waxed paper; if using waxed paper, spread with ghee first.

Lay out ground meat in the middle in the form of a rectangle 1 cm thick. Place eggs in the middle, then roll meat over eggs and seal edges. Place in a rectangular baking pan.

6. Place in a medium hot oven for 30 minutes. Pour 1/2 cup water into pan during cooking.

7. Remove waxed paper and slice kufta roll into 2 cm thick slices. Do not remove omentum. Serve hot.

Dawud Pasha Kufta

Ingredients

1 onion
Salt and pepper
1/4 teaspoon nutmeg
Mixed spice
1 kilogram ground beef
2 tablespoons ghee
2 cloves garlic
1 cup tomato juice
1 cup meat broth

Method

1. Finely grate onion. Season with salt, pepper, nutmeg, and mixed spice. Mix well with ground meat and shape into small, marble-sized balls.

2. Melt ghee in a skillet over medium heat. Add kufta, stirring occasionally until browned on all sides. Remove from ghee.

3. Crush garlic and saute in remaining ghee. Add tomato juice, salt and pepper and cook until sauce thickens.

4. Add broth and bring to a boil. Return kufta and bring to boil. Lower heat and simmer until sauce thickens and ghee rises to the top. Serve.

Breaded Fried Kufta

Ingredients
1 onion
1/2 kilogram ground beef
2 eggs
1 tablespoon chopped parsley
Salt and pepper
1/2 teaspoon mixed spice
1 cup fine dried bread crumbs
2 tablespoons ghee for frying
Parsley sprigs for garnish

Method

1. Finely grate onion. Combine with meat, 1 egg, parsley, salt, pepper, and mixed spice. Combine all ingredients well and set aside for at least 30 minutes.

2. Shape meat mixture into circular patties. Beat other egg with a little salt and pepper. Coat meat patties with egg, then with bread crumbs.

3. Deep fry in hot ghee or oil (about 5 cm deep). Serve hot on a plate, garnished with parsley.

Rice Kufta with Tomato Sauce and Chickpeas

Ingredients

1 cup chickpeas
1 kilogram fried rice kufta
    (page 132)
1 onion
1 tablespoon corn oil
2 cloves garlic
1 cup tomato juice
Salt and pepper
1 liter meat broth
1 tablespoon dried mint

Method

1. Soak chickpeas in water for 2 hours. Boil in water for 30 minutes.

2. Prepare rice kufta and fry. Set aside. Fry whole onion in hot oil until golden yellow. Add garlic whole, and fry. Add tomato juice seasoned with salt and pepper and simmer until sauce thickens.

3. Add meat broth and bring to a boil. Add fried kufta and boiled chickpeas and boil for 30 minutes. Lower heat and simmer for 15   minutes until sauce thickens. Sprinkle with dried mint and serve.

Meat and Kufta in Sour Sauce *(Hamid)*

Ingredients

2 bunches chard
1 large onion
1 1/2 liters water
Salt and pepper
1/2 kilogram meat cubes
1/2 kilogram rice kufta
    (page 132)
1/2 cup rice
Juice of 6 limes
4 cloves garlic, crushed
1 bunch fresh coriander,
    chopped
1/4 cup corn oil

Method

1. Remove leaves from chard and set aside. Chop onion and chard stems. Fry onion until golden yellow, then add chard stems and fry until yellowish.

2. Add water, salt and pepper and bring to a boil. Add meat cubes and kufta and cook for 30 minutes or until meat is well done.

3. Remove kufta and meat from liquid and add rice. Bring to a boil.

4. In a separate saucepan, boil chard leaves in a little water and blend. Add to rice mixture. Add lime juice. Boil until mixture thickens, and return the cooked meat to the pot. Serve in a deep dish.

5. Arrange kufta balls on top of serving dish. Saute crushed garlic and coriander in oil. Sprinkle over top. Serve.

Poultry and Rabbit

There are Two Types of Domesticated Birds:

1. Those with **white meat**, such as chickens and turkey.
2. Those with **dark meat**, such as ducks, geese, and pigeons.

Note that birds that have white meat are easier to digest, as they are lower in fat.

There are Several Types of Chickens:

• **White farm chickens** are usually slaughtered at a young age as they reach the weight of 1–1 1/2 kilograms by the age of 1–1 1/2 months. Their meat is white in color and not very high in fats. It is tender and does not require prolonged cooking; usually 30 minutes is enough for a medium chicken.

• **Red farm chickens** have the same characteristics as white chickens, but are a hybrid of the white farm chickens and the local *(baladi)* chickens.

• *Baladi* **(local) chickens** are smaller in size and have multicolored feathers. Baladi chickens are either slaughtered at the age of 6 months, which are known as

bidara or at the older age of one year, known as *'atqia*.

There are Two Kinds of Wild Birds:

• **Migrant birds** that come from Europe during the fall and are caught by hunters in nets that are set up along the seashore. These are smaller in size and tend to have tougher meat.

Pintail ducks are migrant birds. They resemble quails but are larger in size. As they usually do not feed while migrating, they tend to lose most of their fat, leaving meat that is almost fatless and somewhat tough.

• **Farm birds** that are raised by breeders in wire cages. These are larger in size and have a more tender meat.

When Buying Poultry, Make Sure That:

• the eyes are bright
• the beak is flexible and of a bright yellow color
• the breast bone is flexible
• the feathers are shiny and the feathers

- below the wings are small
- the comb is red in color

General Comments about Poultry:

Make sure to remove the crop (the birds stomach) and all the blood that is found clotted inside the bird and embedded in the bone. Also, the chickpea-shaped gland that is found in the tail area must be removed.

It is better to keep the freshly slaughtered bird for 24 hours in the freezer before cooking as this tenderizes the meat, facilitating cutting and cooking.

When cooking a bird in liquid, leave it in the hot broth for five extra minutes after turning off the heat as this makes it more tender.

When frying *baladi* chickens or ducks or other birds that require prolonged cooking, use a skillet with just a shallow layer of ghee as this gives the meat the desired golden brown color without drying it excessively. Roasting poultry requires a longer time and yields a tougher meat. It is therefore preferred to almost completely cook the bird in boiling water before roasting, then to place it in an oven until fully cooked and lightly browned.

When grilling poultry, it is better to marinate the bird in a little oil, lime juice, and yogurt to tenderize the meat. Poultry is usually seasoned with crushed garlic, salt, pepper, thyme, and rosemary as well as oil, lime juice, and yogurt. Allow poultry to marinate for at least 3 hours before grilling.

Geese must also be soaked in water and vinegar to loosen their fat.

As for wild ducks, it is preferable to boil them first for 5 minutes, drain, then boil them again in fresh water, adding the usual spices (4 mastic grains, 4 cardamom pods, 2 bay leaves and a punch of celery, carrot, and leek.) This is done to get rid of the fishy odor found in wild ducks, which feed on fish.

Rabbits

Rabbits must be cut into quarters and left to soak in cold, salted water for 30 minutes before boiling.

Boiled and Roasted Turkey
(Dindi)

Ingredients

Ingredients
1 turkey (6–8 kilograms)
4 liters water
1 carrot
1 large onion
3–4 mastic grains
3–4 cardamom pods
Salt and pepper
Bay leaf
2 celery sticks
2 tablespoons ghee
1 recipe *khalta* rice (page 236)

Method

1. Clean the turkey. Remove head, neck, and tips of wings. Use a piece of string to tie the thighs against the bird. (Remove the string after boiling)

2. Boil water in a large cooking pot. Add bird, carrot, and onion and boil for a few minutes. Remove froth as it forms. Add mastic, cardamom, pepper, bay leaf and celery.

3. Cook for 2–2 1/2 hours. Poke the thick areas of the bird with a knife to ensure complete cooking. Add salt 5 minutes before bird is fully cooked.

4. Remove turkey from broth. Season with salt and pepper and coat in ghee. Place in a medium hot oven for 30 minutes until golden brown. Cool, then carve into thin slices using a sharp knife.

5. Spoon khalta rice in a large round or oval serving dish. Arrange turkey slices on top of rice.

6. Add 1 cup broth to the drippings left in the oven pan. Boil for a few minutes, then spoon over turkey and rice.

Note: You may serve the bird whole to be carved on the table.

Turkey with Khalta Rice

Method

1. Prepare nuts: in ghee, lightly fry the almonds, pistachios, and pine nuts separately. Fry the raisins until they become puffy. Fry the chicken livers.

2. Soak rice in water for 1 hour. Drain. Fry in ghee for a few minutes. Add broth, salt, and pepper and bring to a boil. Add nuts, stir and cook for 15 minutes until liquid is absorbed. Stir and cool.

3. Wash turkey and prepare for cooking. Stuff with the prepared rice mix and season from the outside with salt and pepper. Place in a large oven pan and coat with ghee. Season with rosemary and bay leaf and place in a hot oven to roast. From time to time, add 1 cup broth to the pan and baste with drippings until fully cooked and golden brown in color. Approximate cooking time is 3–4 hours depending on size.

Ingredients

Khalta Rice:
1/2 cup ghee
1 1/2 cups boiled peeled almonds
1 1/2 cups shelled pistachios
1 1/2 cups pine nuts
1/2 cup raisins
1/2 kilogram chicken livers
1 kilogram rice
2 liters broth
Salt and pepper

1 turkey (6–8 kilograms)
1 tablespoon rosemary
Bay leaf
Tomato or lime slices, for garnish

4. Allow the turkey to cool a little, then carve with a sharp knife. Arrange on an oval plate garnished with tomato or lime slices. Serve.

5. Add 1 cup broth to the drippings left in the oven tray. Boil, drain and serve the sauce in a bowl next to the turkey.

Roasted Duck

Ingredients

Duck (male)
(2 1/2 kilograms)
2 liters water
1 onion
3–4 mastic grains
3–4 cardamom pods
Bay leaf
Salt and pepper
2 tablespoons ghee

Method

1. Clean duck and wash well from the inside and outside. Remove any blood clots from the cavity and remove the gland at the tail.

2. Boil water and add duck and whole onion. Bring to a boil, removing any froth that forms. Add mastic grains, cardamom, bay leaf, and pepper.

3. Poke breast in several places to ensure complete cooking and continue cooking for 1 1/2 hours until almost cooked. Add salt. Remove any froth that forms.

4. Remove pot from heat. Leave the duck in the hot broth for 5 minutes, then remove and place in an oven pan. Season with salt and pepper and coat with ghee. Place in a medium hot oven for about 1 hour until duck is fully cooked and top is lightly browned.

5. Serve duck with *khalta* rice (recipe, page 143) or with a pan of *ruqaq* filled with ground beef (see recipe, page 252).

Roasted Goose

Ingredients

1 large goose (about 4
  kilograms)
2 liters water
1/4 cup vinegar
1 onion
3–4 mastic grains
3–4 cardamom pods
Bay leaf
Salt and pepper
2 tablespoons ghee

Method

1. Clean goose. Soak in
   water with vinegar for
   30 minutes before
   cooking.

2. Cook goose in the
   same way as duck in
   previous recipe. Serve
   with *khalta* rice (page
   143) or *ruqaq* (page
   252).

Fried Whole Chicken

Method

1. Clean chicken and tie legs by placing them inside the lower opening of the chicken so that it holds its shape. Heat 1 tablespoon ghee in a large, deep pot. Lightly fry whole onion in ghee, then add mastic grains, and a little pepper. Add chicken and fry on all sides until a light golden color.

2. Add water and boil, adding cardamom and bay leaf. Cook until well done, around 30 minutes, adding salt 5 minutes before the end of cooking.

3. Leave chicken in hot broth for 5 minutes, away from heat.

4. Remove chicken from broth and season with salt and pepper.

5. Heat remaining ghee. Fry chicken over high heat, turning until golden brown on all sides. Serve.

Note: Instead of frying chicken, you can coat with ghee and placed it in a medium hot oven until it is golden brown.

Ingredients

Ingredients
1 medium chicken (around 1 1/2 kilograms)
2 tablespoons ghee
1 onion
2 mastic grains
Salt and pepper
1 liter water
3–4 cardamom pods
Bay leaf

Grilled Chicken

Ingredients

1 small white farm chicken
(3/4–1 kilogram)
4 cloves garlic
1 tablespoon oil
1 tablespoon lime juice
1 cup yogurt
Salt and pepper
1 tablespoon thyme
1 tablespoon rosemary
1 tomato
Parsley sprigs

Method

1. Clean chicken well. Cut through backbone to flatten chicken and pound with a meat mallet. Wash well. Use a sharp knife to make several slits in the meat to allow good marination.

2. Crush garlic and combine with oil, lime juice, yogurt, salt, pepper, thyme, and rosemary. Peel tomato, blend in blender and stir into garlic mixture. Use to season chicken. Allow chicken to marinate for at least 1 hour.

3. Grill chicken over coals or using a double grill (a grill with a cover and a pot beneath it to catch liquid resulting from the grilling process). Baste frequently with marinade so that chicken retains its moisture. Serve on a plate, garnished with parsley and with french fries or sauteed vegetables on the side.

Chicken Casserole with Rice
(Bram dagag bi-l-urz)

Ingredients
2 cups rice
1 teaspoon salt
1 liter water
1 medium chicken (1 1/2 kilograms)
2 tablespoons ghee
Salt and pepper
1/4 teaspoon nutmeg
3 cups milk
2 tablespoons cream

Method

1. Wash rice, add 1 teaspoon salt to 1 liter water and soak rice for 1 hour.

2. Cut chicken into 8 pieces and wash well.

3. Coat the bottom and sides of a large earthenware container *(bram)* with ghee.

4. Strain rice and spoon half the amount into the container. Arrange the chicken pieces on top, then cover with the remaining rice. Season with salt, pepper, and a little nutmeg.

5. Boil milk. Add to rice and bake in a hot oven for 30 minutes until liquid is absorbed. Bring *bram* out of oven, spoon cream onto top and return to medium hot oven for 5 minutes until top is browned. Serve.

Ingredients
1 medium white farm chicken (1 1/2 kilograms)
2 tomatoes
2 sweet peppers
1/4 kilogram pearl onions
Parsley
Marinade:
4 cloves garlic
1 tablespoon oil
1 tablespoon lime juice
1 cup yogurt
Salt and pepper
1 tablespoon thyme
1 tablespoon rosemary
1 tomato

Chicken Kebabs

Method

1. Remove skin and bones from chicken. Cut into one inch cubes.

2. Season chicken (with marinade ingredients) in same way as Step 2 in grilled chicken (page 148). Marinate for at least 1 hour.

3. Cut 2 tomatoes and 2 peppers into cubes. Peel pearl onions.

4. Thread chicken cubes on skewers, alternating between chicken and vegetable cubes (tomato, sweet pepper, onion).

5. Grill on both sides for about 10 minutes. Brush frequently with marinade, using a brush or parsley stems.

6. Remove from skewers and place on a plate garnished with parsley. Serve.

Sharkasia Chicken

Ingredients

1 baladi chicken
   (1 1/2–2 kilograms)
2 tablespoons ghee
4 cups chicken broth
1 teaspoon salt
4 cups rice
1 recipe sharkasia sauce
   (below)

Method

1. Boil chicken and fry as in Fried Whole Chicken, page 147. Divide into quarters.

2. Heat ghee. Add broth and salt and bring to a boil.

3. Wash rice and add. Boil, then simmer over low heat for 15 minutes until fully cooked.

4. Spoon rice onto a large round plate. Create a well in the center of the rice and pour the sharkasia sauce into the well. Arrange pieces of fried chicken around rice and serve hot.

Sharkasia Sauce

Ingredients

1/4 kilogram walnuts
1 medium onion
2 tablespoons ghee
1 cup chicken broth
Salt and pepper
Pulp of 1 baguette
2 cloves garlic
1 tablespoon dried
   coriander

Method

1. Soak walnuts in water for 10 minutes and slip the skins off the nutmeats.

2. Grate onion and saute lightly in ghee until golden yellow. Add 1 cup broth, salt, and pepper, and bring to a boil.

3. Soak bread pulp in a little broth. Squeeze out excess liquid, add to walnuts, and process in a food processor until mixture has a paste-like consistency. Add to boiling broth and cook over low heat for a few minutes.

4. Crush garlic and coriander. Fry in a little ghee and add to above mixture. Serve with chicken.

Chicken Kishk *(Kishk almaz bi-l-dagag)*

Ingredients

1 cup yogurt
1/2 cup flour
1 cup milk
1 onion
1/4 cup corn oil
2 cups chicken broth
2 cloves garlic, crushed
Salt and pepper
1 medium chicken, boiled,
    deboned, and cut into
    small pieces

Method

1. Mix yogurt and flour. Add milk and blend. Strain, cover and set aside for about 1 hour.

2. Grate onion and saute lightly in oil until golden yellow. Remove from heat.

3. In a separate saucepan, boil broth. Add crushed garlic, salt, and pepper and boil for 5 minutes.

4. Add yogurt mixture, stirring constantly, until it thickens.

5. Add chicken to boiling mixture along with 1 tablespoon of the golden fried onions.

6. Pour mixture into a deep serving dish. Decorate top with remaining fried onions and oil leftover from frying the onions. Serve.

Note: *Kishk* is a thick creamy sauce, which can be served warm but is usually served cold.

Upper Egyptian Kishk *(Kishk Sa'idi)*

Method

1. Soak the *kishk* in water for about 4 hours, changing the water frequently to get rid of the *kishk's* strong odor. Strain *kishk* from water.

2. Boil broth. Add *kishk* to broth and cook for 15 minutes.

3. In a separate saucepan, saute onion in ghee until yellow in color. Add garlic and stir a little.

4. Add tomato juice and cook over medium heat until sauce thickens and ghee rises to the top. Add tomato-garlic mixture to boiling *kishk* and continue cooking for about 15 minutes or until well done.

5. Dissolve flour in water. Add to *kishk*, stirring constantly until mixture thickens. Season with salt and pepper. Serve.

Ingredients

1/4 kilogram prepared kishk

2 cups chicken broth

1 medium onion, grated

2 tablespoons ghee

4 cloves garlic, crushed

1 cup tomato juice

1/2 cup flour

1/2 cup water

Salt and pepper

Note: *Kishk Sa'idi* is consisting of green cracked wheat and buttermilk which are kneaded together. The mixture is then divided into egg-sized balls that are left out in the sun for 5 days or until very dry. The balls are then stored until needed.

Stuffed Fried Chicken *(Dagag mahshi)*

Method

1. Grate onion. Dice chicken livers and gizzards. Season with salt and pepper. Wash rice and add to liver and gizzard mix. Add 1/2 tablespoon ghee and mix all ingredients well.

2. Clean and wash chicken. Stuff with above mixture from the bottom and close opening using a needle and thread.

3. Boil water. Add stuffed chicken and boil, removing froth as it forms.

4. Add mastic grains, cardamom, and bay leaf and continue cooking around 30 minutes until well done. Remove from heat. Leave chicken in hot broth for 5 minutes, then remove. Season with salt and pepper.

5. Fry chicken in a skillet in a little ghee until golden brown. Serve.

Ingredients

1 large onion

1/4 kilogram chicken livers and gizzards

Salt and pepper

1 cup rice

1 tablespoon ghee

1 medium (farm) chicken

1 1/2 liters water

3–4 mastic grains

3–4 cardamom pods

Bay leaf

Stuffed Pigeons

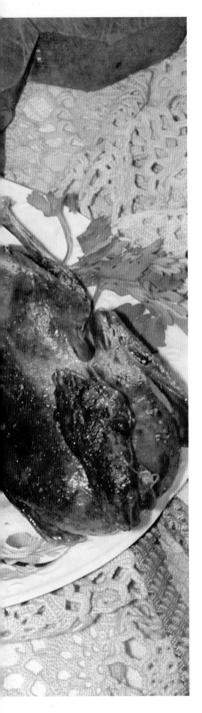

Method

1. Clean the cracked wheat then soak it in hot water for at least 1 hour.

2. Grate onions and season with salt and pepper. Dice livers and gizzards.

3. Strain cracked wheat and add to above mixture. Add 1/2 tablespoon ghee. Mix well.

4. Wash pigeons well. Stuff with the above mixture from the bottom, then close using a needle and thread. Some stuffing can also be added under the skin in the neck and breast areas.

5. Boil water and add pigeons. Remove froth as it forms.

6. Add mastic grains, cardamom, and bay leaf. Cook over medium heat until well done (about 1 hour). Remove from heat and leave 5 minutes in hot broth. Remove.

Ingredients
1 cup cracked wheat
2 onions
Salt and pepper
Livers and gizzards of 6 pigeons
1 tablespoon ghee
6 large pigeons
1 1/2 liters water
3–4 mastic grains
3–4 cardamom pods
Bay leaf

7. Season pigeons with salt and pepper. Coat with ghee and bake in a hot oven for 15 minutes until golden brown. Serve.

Note: You may use rice instead of cracked wheat.

Pigeon and Cracked Wheat Casserole

Method

1. After cleaning cracked wheat, soak in hot water for about 1 hour.

2. Coat bottom and sides of *bram* with ghee. Spoon half of the cracked wheat into the container.

3. Place pigeons whole or cut into quarters. Add remaining cracked wheat and season with salt and pepper.

4. Add broth and place *bram*, covered, in a hot oven for 1 hour.

5. Remove cover and bake in oven for 5 minutes more, until top is golden brown.

Note: You may use rice instead of cracked wheat. Soak rice in salt water for a while before use.

Ingredients

1 cup cracked wheat

1 tablespoon ghee

2 large pigeons

Salt and pepper

1 cup chicken broth

Stewed and Fried Pigeons

Method

1. Clean pigeons and wash well.

2. Heat ghee. Add mastic grains and a little pepper. Fry pigeons, turning on all sides until browned. Cover and cook over low heat, stirring occasionally. Season with salt.

3. Add a little broth if needed and continue cooking until liquid is absorbed and birds are browned on all sides and fully cooked. Serve.

Ingredients

4 medium pigeons

1 tablespoon ghee

2 mastic grains

Salt and pepper

1/2 cup broth

Grilled Pigeons

Ingredients

4 large pigeons
2 cloves garlic
Salt and pepper
1 tablespoon thyme
1 tablespoon rosemary
Juice of 1 lime
1/4 cup corn oil
1 cup yogurt
Parsley, for garnish

Method

1. Clean pigeons and wash well. Cut along backbone and flatten bird by beating a little with a meat mallet.

2. Crush garlic and mix with salt, pepper, thyme, rosemary, lime juice, oil, and yogurt. Rub mixture onto pigeons and marinate for at least 1 hour.

3. Grill over coals or on a double grill. Brush on marinade frequently to prevent drying and grill for about 10 minutes. Do not over grill. Serve on a plate, garnished with parsley.

Fried Quails

Grilled Quails

Ingredients

6 quails
1 tablespoon ghee
2 mastic grains
Salt and pepper

Method

1. Clean and wash quails. Pat dry.

2. Heat ghee. Add mastic grains and pepper. Add quails and fry, turning on all sides until golden brown. Cover and cook over low heat for 30 minutes, stirring occasionally. Season with salt.

3. When liquid is absorbed, continue cooking in remaining ghee until browned on all sides. Serve.

Ingredients

6 quails
Juice of 1 onion, grated
Salt and pepper
1 tablespoon thyme
1 tablespoon rosemary
2 tablespoons oil
Juice of 1/2 lime

Method

1. Clean and wash quails. Cut open along back and pound.

2. Marinate with onion juice, salt, pepper, thyme, rosemary, oil, and lime juice. Cover and set aside for at least 1 hour.

3. Grill over coals for 10 minutes, brushing frequently with marinade. Serve hot.

Quails in Tomato Sauce

Ingredients
6 quails
1 large onion
1 tablespoon ghee
Salt and pepper
1 cup tomato juice

Method

1. Clean quails and wash well.

2. In large sauce pan, grate onion and saute lightly in ghee until golden yellow. Add quails and a little pepper.

3. Cook quails in covered saucepan over medium heat, stirring from time to time until liquid is absorbed.

4. Add tomato juice and salt. Cook over low heat until sauce thickens and ghee rises to the top. Serve.

Quails with Rice

Ingredients
2 cups rice
6 quails
1 onion
1 tablespoon ghee
2 1/2 cups chicken broth
Salt and pepper

Method

1. Wash rice and soak in cold water.

2. Clean quails and wash well.

3. Grate onion and saute lightly in ghee until golden yellow. Add quails and stir until lightly browned.

4. Add broth. Season with salt and pepper and boil for a few minutes. Strain rice, add to pot with quails and bring to a boil over medium heat.

5. When liquid is absorbed, lower heat and continue cooking until rice is fully cooked. Serve.

Fried Fagafig Birds

Ingredients
12 fagafig (small, sparrow-like) birds
1 tablespoon ghee
2 mastic grains
Salt and pepper

Method

1. Clean and wash birds well.

2. Heat ghee. Add mastic grains, then birds. Stir and season with salt and pepper. Cover and cook over low heat, stirring occasionally until liquid is absorbed.

3. Continue stirring in remaining ghee until evenly browned. Serve.

Fagafig Birds with Rice

Ingredients

Ingredients
2 cups rice
1 onion
1 tablespoon ghee
12 fagafig birds
2 1/2 cups broth
Salt and pepper

Method

1. Wash rice and soak in cold water for 1 hour.

2. Grate onion and lightly saute in ghee until golden yellow. Add birds and stir.

3. Add broth and season with salt and pepper. Bring to a boil, strain rice, then add to broth.

4. Bring rice to a boil over medium heat, then lower heat and simmer until rice is fully cooked. Serve.

Pintail Duck with Marta Seasoning

Ingredients

Ingredients
4 pintail ducks
2 large onions
Salt and pepper
1 tablespoon cumin
Livers and gizzards of the ducks
1 cup rice
1 liter water
3–4 mastic grains
3–4 cardamom pods
Bay leaf
2 tablespoons ghee

Method

1. Clean and wash birds well inside and outside. Place in boiling water for 5 minutes, then remove them.

2. Grate onion and season with salt, pepper, and cumin. Dice the livers and gizzards and add to seasoned onion mixture. Wash rice and add to mixture.

3. Stuff birds with the above mixture and use needle and thread to close lower opening.

4. Boil water and add stuffed birds. Remove froth as it forms. Add mastic grains, cardamom, and bay leaf and continue cooking until well done.

5. Remove from heat, but leave birds in hot broth for 5 minutes.

6. Remove birds from broth. Season them with salt and pepper and fry in a skillet in ghee, stirring, until evenly browned on all sides. Serve.

Wild Duck

Ingredients

2 wild ducks

1 1/2 liters water

2 large onions

Salt and pepper

1 tablespoon cumin

Livers and gizzards of
the ducks

1 cup rice

3–4 mastic grains

3–4 cardamom pods

Bay leaf

2 tablespoons ghee

Method

1. Clean and wash birds well inside and outside with soap and water. Place in boiling water for 5 minutes, then remove them.

2. Discard water and wash ducks again with fresh water.

3. Grate onion and season with salt, pepper, and cumin. Dice the livers and gizzards and add to seasoned onion mixture. Wash rice and add to mixture. Stuff birds with the above mixture and use needle and thread to close lower opening.

4. Cook by boiling in water with mastic, cardamom, and bay leaf, then frying quickly in a skillet in hot ghee. Serve.

Boiled and Fried Rabbit

Method

1. Skin rabbit and remove guts. Wash well inside and outside. Cut into 5 pieces and soak in salted water for 15 minutes, then rinse.

2. Boil water. Add rabbit and whole onion.

3. Remove froth as it forms. Add mastic grains, cardamom, bay leaf, and pepper. Boil for around 45 minutes, then add salt. Remove from heat and leave in broth for 5 minutes.

Ingredients

1 medium rabbit (1 1/2
kilograms)

1 1/2 liters water

1 onion

3–4 mastic grains

3–4 cardamom pods

Bay leaf

Salt and pepper

2 tablespoons ghee

4. Remove rabbit pieces and season with salt and pepper. Fry in ghee until golden brown. Serve.

Seafood

Fish are a highly nutritious and easily digested food and fish contain significant quantities of phosphorous, protein, and beneficial oils.

Fish are low in calories and have none of the saturated fats that are difficult to digest. The fat content of seabass, crabs, sibia (squid), and shrimp is 2%, while gray mullet and eels are more than 6% fat. One hundred grams of fish contain approximately 100 calories; in comparison, 100 grams of meat contain 300. The small amount of fat in fish helps us to maintain low blood cholesterol levels and is sufficient to give the body the fat it needs for healthy skin and hair.

Studies have proven that people can meet their requirements of vitamins A and D from fish oil, which is a rich source of these vitamins. These vitamins are also present in large amounts in fish roe (caviar). Vitamin B complex is found in the skins of some fish in amounts equal to those found in meats.

Fish are a storage depot for phosphorous and some other minerals that help raise the intelligence level. The presence of phosphorous is essential for the absorption of vitamin B complex. The iron present in fish helps with the production and maintenance of red blood cells (hemoglobin), while the iodine helps stimulate and maintain the thyroid.

Egypt has a wide variety of fish sources, from both seas and rivers. Almost all known Red Sea and Mediterranean fish, shellfish, and mussels, as well as freshwater fish from riversand lakes, are available in Egyptian markets.

Generally, fish can be divided into two kinds:

Saltwater fish (from seas and oceans). These are characterized by their large size and thick scales. They usually have white, low-fat meat. Those most commonly found in Egypt include: seabass, bluefish, gray mullet, seaperch, sole, red mullet, squirrel fish, sea bream, eel, sardines, sibia (squid), octopus, ray fish, trigle, and silver-sided fish. Also commonly found are shellfish such as shrimps, crabs, oysters, and mussels.

Freshwater fish (from rivers and lakes). These tend to be smaller in size and have delicate, dark-colored meat that is higher in fat. Several types are found in Egypt, including the Nile bass, gray mullet, eel, tilapia, grouper, catfish, and Nile perch.

There are now fish farms for breeding fish and shellfish, particularly for tilapia, mullet, and shrimp.

There are Three Types of Shrimp

Blue jumbo prawns (*kazaz*) are large with a translucent shell. They are usually grilled.

Red shrimp are medium-sized. They are used for casseroles, rice, stewing, and frying.

White shrimp are usually small. They are used in making shrimp kufta, kamuniya casserole and in rice.

There are Two Types of Crabs

Blue crabs (males) have long, strong claws and firm meat.

Red crabs (females) are smaller and have smaller claws, more tender meat and contain the roe (eggs).

Note: Males and females can be distinguished by the triangle shape on the bottom shell, which is long and thin in males and short and wide in females.

Other Seafood

Sibia (squid) are medium in size and have a flat body.

Calamari have a long, narrow body. May be medium or large.

Octopus are large and have eight tentacles.

Smoked herring and salted cod are two types of imported fish that are very popular in Egypt. Salted cod must be soaked in water for 24 hours before using. The water must be changed every 6 hours.

Advice When Buying Fresh Fish

• The fish skin must be tight and shiny.

• When pressed with the fingers, the flesh of the fish should spring back, leaving no indentation.

• Fish must be have a fresh odor, similar to that of seawater.

• Eyes must be clear and shiny, not sunken.

• Gills must be a rose-red color with no grayish tinge.

• It is better to buy fish the day it will be eaten. Avoid storing fish in a freezer for more than one week.

• When buying oysters or mussels, the outside shells must be closed and not easily opened, which indicates freshness.

Grilled Fish with Bran

Ingredients

1 kilogram gray mullet
   or tilapia
Salt and pepper
1 large cup bran
4 cloves garlic
1 tablespoon cumin
1/2 tablespoon red pepper
1 tablespoon lime juice
Lime halves

Method

1. Wash fish well. Wash gills without removing. Don't remove guts or scales.

2. Season fish with salt and pepper. Coat with bran. Grill fish well on both sides until fully cooked (around 30 minutes).

3. Crush unpeeled garlic together with salt, cumin, and red pepper. Mix in a little water. Add lime juice.

4. Remove fish from grill and place immediately in garlic mixture for 1 minute. Place in a colander to discard excess water, and sprinkle with salt and pepper. Arrange on a plate and serve with lime halves.

Note: Serve with white rice cooked in oil instead of ghee

167

Grilled Fish with Oil and Lime

Ingredients
1 kilogram perch fillet or large red mullet
Salt and pepper
Bay leaf
1 tablespoon rosemary
1/2 cup corn oil
1 tablespoon lime juice
Parsley sprigs
Lime slices

Method

1. Clean the fish by removing guts and gills, and wash it well. Season with salt, pepper, bay leaf, rosemary, oil, and lime juice. Marinate for 30 minutes.

2. Heat a Teflon skillet and spray or brush with oil. Place fish on skillet and cook, brushing frequently with marinade. Flip onto other side and continue cooking and brushing with marinade until golden brown.

3. Serve on a plate, garnished with parsley and lime slices.

Fried Fish

Ingredients

1 kilogram fish (red
   mullet, sole, tilapia,
   or any fish fillet)
2 cloves garlic
Salt and pepper
1 tablespoon cumin
Juice of 1 lime
1/2 cup flour
Oil for deep frying
Parsley sprigs
Lime slices

Method

1. Clean fish well. Remove gills and guts, scrape scales, then rinse well with water.

2. Crush garlic together with salt, pepper, and cumin. Add lime juice and cover fish well with the mixture both inside and outside. Marinate fish for 1 hour.

3. Coat fish with flour on both sides and shake off any extra flour.

4. Deep fry fish on both sides in hot oil (about 5 cm deep) until golden brown. Remove from oil and serve on a plate, garnished with parsley and lime slices.

Fried Fish with Tomato Sauce and Garlic

Ingredients

1 kilogram tilapia or sole

Salt and pepper

1/4 cup flour

Oil for deep frying

4 cloves garlic

1 tablespoon oil

1 cup tomato juice

1/4 cup vinegar

Method

1. Clean fish well and season with salt and pepper. Cover with flour then deep fry in oil (about 5 cm deep). Arrange in a serving dish.

2. Crush garlic and saute lightly in 1 tablespoon oil until yellow. Add tomato juice and cook until sauce thickens and oil rises to the top.

3. Add vinegar and boil for a few minutes. Pour over fried fish and set aside for a short while until the sauce is absorbed by the fish. Serve.

Fisherman's Style Fish

Ingredients

1 kilogram gray mullet or
catfish
1 large onion
1 tablespoon corn oil
2 tablespoons water
1 liter water
Salt and pepper
1 tablespoon cumin
3–4 mastic grains
3–4 cardamom pods
2 cups rice

Method

1. Clean and wash fish. Cut into medium pieces (about 10 cm in length).

2. Grate onion and saute in oil until dark brown in color. Add 2 tablespoons water and stir well until onion loosens completely. Add 1 liter water and bring to a boil.

3. Add salt, pepper, cumin, mastic, and cardamom. Add fish and boil for 10 minutes. Remove fish and place in a deep bowl and cover.

4. Using 2 cups of the broth, cook the rice.

5. Spoon cooked rice onto a round serving dish. Arrange fish around the rice. Serve. Serve the broth in a deep bowl beside the rice and fish.

172

Fish with Coriander

Method

1. Wash fish and clean well. Cut into pieces, season with salt, pepper, cumin, and 2 crushed garlic cloves, and set aside for 15 minutes. Cover with flour and deep fry in oil (about 5 cm deep) until light golden brown.

2. Grate onions and saute in oil until yellow. Crush the 2 remaining garlic cloves, and add with coriander to onion. Stir for a short while.

3. Add tomato juice and season with salt, pepper, and fish spice. Cook until sauce thickens and oil rises to the top.

4. Add water to onion and tomato mixture and bring to a boil.

5. Place fish in an oven tray and pour the onion mixture over it. Bake in a medium hot oven for about 10 minutes or until top is golden brown. Serve.

Ingredients

1 kilogram grouper or gray mullet
Salt and pepper
4 cloves garlic
2 tablespoons cumin
1/2 cup flour
Oil for deep frying
4 onions
2 tablespoons corn oil
2 tablespoons crushed dried coriander
2 cups tomato juice
1 tablespoon fish spice
1 cup water

Fish and Potato Casserole

Ingredients

1 kilogram fish (bluefish, gray mullet or seabass)
1 garlic head
2 hot chili peppers
1 bunch celery, chopped
Salt and pepper
Juice of 4 limes
1 kilogram potatoes
1 tomato, sliced
2 limes, sliced
1 sweet pepper, sliced
1/4 cup corn oil
1/2 cup water

Method

1. Clean and wash fish well. Remove guts and gills.

2. Crush garlic, hot peppers, and celery. Add salt, pepper, and lime juice.

3. Using a knife, make a lengthwise slit along the back of the fish. Stuff back and belly with about 2/3 of the garlic mixture.

4. Cut potatoes into medium slices and season with remaining garlic mixture and salt and pepper.

5. Arrange potatoes in an oven tray. Arrange fish on top of potatoes and cover with slices of tomato, lime, and sweet pepper. Drizzle the oil over the whole tray.

6. Add water to the fish and bake in a hot oven for 30 minutes until top is lightly browned. Serve.

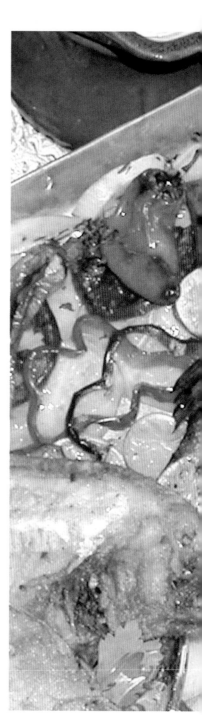

Greek-style Grilled Fish *(Samak singari)*

Ingredients

Ingredients
1 kilogram perch or gray mullet or bass
1 head garlic
4 tomatoes
4 hot chili peppers
4 limes
1 bunch celery, chopped
Salt and pepper
3 tablespoons corn oil
Juice of 4 limes
1/2 cup water

Method

1. Clean fish and wash. Using a sharp knife, cut open the belly side all the way through and lay the fish out flat. Remove spine.

2. Crush garlic, dice tomatoes and hot peppers, and thinly slice limes. Mix with chopped celery and season with salt and pepper.

3. Place fish in an oven pan. Cover with seasoning mix and sprinkle with oil and lime juice. Add water to the pan.

4. Place in hot oven for 30 minutes or until cooked and top is lightly browned. Serve.

Fried Salted Cod *(Samak bakalah maqli)*

Ingredients
1 kilogram salted cod
4 cloves garlic
Salt and pepper
1 tablespoon cumin
1 tablespoon lime juice
1/2 cup flour
Oil for deep frying
Parsley sprigs
1 lime slice

Method

1. Soak fish in water for 24 hours, changing the water every 6 hours.

2. Slice fish, wash, and season with crushed garlic, salt, pepper, cumin, and lime juice.

3. Coat in flour. Deep fry in hot oil (about 5 cm deep) and serve on a plate, garnished with parsley and lime slices.

Fried Salted Cod in Tomato Sauce *(Samak bakalah bi-l-salsa)*

Ingredients
1 kilogram salted cod
1 large onion
1 tablespoon oil
4 cloves garlic
1 cup tomato sauce
Salt and pepper
1 bunch parsley, chopped
1 cup water

Method

1. Soak, season, and fry fish as in previous recipe.

2. Grate onion and saute lightly in oil until yellow. Add garlic, chopped, and continue cooking until garlic is a golden brown color. Add tomato sauce and season with salt and pepper. Cook over medium heat until sauce thickens and oil rises to the top.

3. Add 1 cup water to tomato sauce and bring to a boil.

4. Arrange fish in an oven dish, pour tomato sauce mixture over fish, add parsley, and bake in a medium hot oven for 10 minutes. Serve.

Fish with Celery Casserole

Ingredients

1 kilogram fish fillet
   (perch or bass)
Salt and pepper
1/2 cup flour
Oil for deep frying
2 large onions
6 cloves garlic
4 tomatoes
1 hot chili pepper
2 limes
1 bunch celery
1/2 cup corn oil
1/2 cup water
Lime slices

Method

1. Clean fish and slice into 1 inch thick slices. Season with salt and pepper. Coat in flour and half cook by deep frying in hot oil (about 5 cm deep). Arrange in oven dish.

2. Slice onions, garlic, tomatoes, hot pepper, and limes. Finely chop celery.

3. Fry onion in corn oil until yellow in color. Add garlic and stir, then add celery and chopped pepper and continue stirring.

4. Add tomato slices and season mixture with salt and pepper. Cook for a few minutes.

5. Add water to the above mixture. Bring to a boil, then pour over fish.

6. Garnish top with lime slices. Bake in a medium hot oven for 15 minutes until fully cooked and top is lightly browned. Serve.

Baked Eels (Samak hinnash fi-l-furn)

Ingredients

Ingredients
1 kilogram eels
4 cloves garlic
Salt and pepper
1 tablespoon cumin
1/2 cup corn oil
1 tablespoon lime juice

Method

1. Skin eels and wash well. Arrange in a round oven pan.

2. Crush garlic and mix with salt, pepper, and cumin. Use to season eels.

3. Add oil and lime juice. Bake in a medium hot oven for around 30 minutes or until fully cooked. Serve.

Fisherman's Style Eel Casserole (Hinnash sayadiya)

Ingredients

Ingredients
1 kilogram eels
Salt and pepper
1 large onion
1/2 cup oil
2 tablespoons water
2 cups water
1 tablespoon cumin
2 cups rice

Method

1. Skin eels and wash well. Season with salt and pepper.

2. Grate onion and saute in oil until brown in color. Add 2 tablespoons water and stir until onion loosens up.

3. Add eels and cook for a few minutes, stirring. Add 2 cups water and season with salt, pepper, and cumin. Bring to a boil and allow eels to cook for 10 minutes, then remove them from the liquid.

4. Add rice to the liquid and bring to a boil. Lower heat and cook until liquid is absorbed. Immerse eel pieces in rice, cover and continue cooking over low heat until fully cooked.

5. Bake in a medium hot oven for 5 minutes until top is browned. Serve.

Fried Eels (Hinnash maqliya)

Ingredients

Ingredients
1 kilogram eels
4 cloves garlic
Salt and pepper
1 teaspoon cumin
2 tablespoons lime juice
Flour
Oil for deep frying

Method

1. Skin eels, cut into pieces, and season with crushed garlic, salt, pepper, cumin, and lime juice.

2. Marinate for 30 minutes. Coat in flour and deep fry in hot oil (about 5 cm deep) on both sides until golden. Serve.

Catfish Casserole with Cracked Wheat
(Tagin qaramit bi-l-firik)

Ingredients

1/4 kilogram cracked wheat
1/2 kilogram onions
1/2 cup corn oil
1 kilogram ripe tomatoes
1 small bunch each, dill, parsley, fresh coriander
1 kilogram large catfish
Oil for deep frying
4 cloves garlic, crushed
Salt and pepper

Method

1. Wash cracked wheat and soak in water for 1 hour.

2. Grate onions and saute in oil until golden yellow. Dice tomatoes, add to mixture, and cook until it thickens and oil rises to the top.

3. Chop dill, parsley, and coriander. Add to tomato mixture and stir.

4. Deep fry catfish in hot oil (about 5 cm deep) until half cooked. Make slit in fish and stuff with garlic and salt.

5. Spoon half the cracked wheat into an oven-proof dish. Arrange catfish on top, then add the remaining cracked wheat. Pour tomato mixture over it, and sprinkle with pepper.

6. Bake in a medium hot oven until liquid is absorbed and top is browned, about 15 minutes. Serve.

Baked Nile Sardines

Ingredients

1 kilogram Nile sardines
1 garlic head
Salt and pepper
1 tablespoon cumin
1 hot chili pepper
1/4 cup corn oil
2 tomatoes, sliced
2 limes, sliced
2 tablespoons oil

Method

1. Wash sardines lightly with water.

2. Crush together garlic, salt, pepper, cumin, and chili pepper.

3. Season sardines with mixture and arrange in an ovenproof dish or pan.

4. Arrange tomato and lime slices over sardines.

5. Sprinkle oil over sardines and place in a hot oven for 15 minutes. Serve.

Fried Sardines

Ingredients
1 kilogram Nile sardines
2 cloves garlic, crushed
Salt and pepper
1 tablespoon cumin
Juice of 1 lime
Flour
Oil for deep frying
Parsley sprigs
Lime slices

Method

1. Wash sardines and season with garlic, salt, pepper, cumin, and lime juice. Marinate for 30 minutes.

2. Coat in flour and deep fry in hot oil (about 5 cm deep) on both sides until golden brown. Serve on a plate, garnished with parsley and lime slices.

Grilled Sardines

Ingredients
1 kilogram Nile sardines
Salt and pepper
2 tablespoons lime juice
1/4 cup oil
1 cup bran
1 tablespoon cumin
Lime slices

Method

1. Wash sardines well but do not remove guts or gills.

2. Season with salt, pepper, 1 tablespoon lime juice and oil. Marinate for 15 minutes.

3. Heat a Teflon pan or an oven pan. Coat sardines in bran and grill quickly on both sides.

4. Season after removing from heat with salt, cumin, and 1 tablespoon lime juice. with lime slices.

Boiled Shrimp

Ingredients
1 kilogram large red shrimp
1 large onion
1 tomato
2 limes
Salt and pepper
2 tablespoons corn oil

Method

1. Wash shrimp well without removing the shells, and place in a colander.

2. Thinly slice onion, tomato, and limes. Season with salt and pepper.

3. Heat oil in a deep cooking pot. Add shrimp and cook for two minutes, shaking pot occasionally to shift shrimp for even cooking. Add sliced vegetables and cover.

4. Cook for 10–15 minutes, shaking pot occasionally.

5. Strain broth left over from cooking. Serve in cups with boiled shrimp.

Grilled Shrimp

Ingredients

1 kilogram jumbo prawns
  (*kazaz*)
4 cloves garlic
1/2 cup corn oil
Juice of 2 limes
Salt and pepper
1 tablespoon fish spice
Lime slices

Method

1. Wash prawns. Using a sharp knife, make a lengthwise slit along the back to remove the vein. Remove shell, leaving only the head and the tail or if pre-ferred, do not remove shell.

2. Crush garlic and add to oil, lime juice, salt, pepper, and fish spice. Mix with prawns in deep plastic container and marinate for at least 1 hour.

3. Heat oven pan well. Arrange shrimp on hot pan and cook, adding marinade occasionally to prevent drying. Flip on other side and repeat. Total cooking time should not exceed 10 minutes.

4. Serve on a plate garnished with lime slices.

Oven Grilled Shrimp

Ingredients

Ingredients
1 kilogram jumbo prawns (*kazaz*)
1 tomato
1 large onion
2 limes
Salt and pepper
2 tablespoons corn oil
Lime slices

Method

1. Wash prawns and slit open back to clean as described in previous recipe.

2. Slice tomato, onion, and limes and season with salt and pepper.

3. Heat oil in metal oven pan. Add shrimp and cook on the stovetop, stirring for 5 minutes.

4. Add seasoned vegetable slices to shrimp. Mix and place in a medium oven for 15 minutes until water is completely absorbed and only oil remains.

5. Serve in a large rectangular dish garnished with lime slices.

Breaded Fried Shrimp

Ingredients

Ingredients
1 kilogram large or medium shrimp
Salt and pepper
1 lime juice
2 eggs
1 cup flour
Oil for deep frying
Lime slices

Method

1. Wash and peel shrimp, and remove heads. Season with salt and pepper, and lime juice.

2. Beat eggs with a fork and season with pepper.

3. Coat shrimp with egg, then with flour.

4. Fry shrimp in hot oil until golden brown. Serve on a plate, garnished with lime slices.

Shrimp with Cumin

Ingredients

Ingredients
1 kilogram medium white shrimp
4 cloves garlic
1 tablespoon cumin
1 tablespoon corn oil
1 cup tomato juice
Salt and pepper

Method

1. Wash and peel shrimp, and remove heads.

2. Crush garlic and mix with cumin. Lightly saute garlic and cumin in oil. Add shrimp and stir for a few minutes.

3. Add tomato juice and season with salt and pepper. Cook until sauce thickens and oil rises to the top. Serve.

Shrimp in Thick Cold Sauce (Kishk gambari)

Ingredients

1/4 cup flour
1 cup yogurt
1/2 cup milk
1 kilogram medium white shrimp
2 tablespoons corn oil
2 cloves garlic
1 cup tomato juice
Salt and pepper
2 cups water or fish broth
A little dried mint

Method

1. Mix flour, yogurt, and milk. Stir well, then strain to ensure that the mixture is not lumpy and that the flour is completely dissolved. Set aside for 1 hour.

2. Peel and wash shrimp well.

3. Lightly saute garlic in oil until yellow in color. Add peeled shrimp and stir a little. Add tomato juice, season with salt and pepper, and cook until sauce thickens and oil rises to the top.

4. Add water or fish broth and bring to a boil. Add yogurt mixture, stirring constantly, until it thickens.

5. Pour into a deep serving dish. Fry mint in a little oil and use to garnish top. Cool a little, then serve.

Shrimp with Green Mallow

Ingredients

1 kilogram medium white
   shrimp
1 kilogram green mallow
   (mulukhiyya), minced
1 liter water
1 onion
Salt and pepper
2 grains mastic
4 cloves garlic
2 tablespoons dried
   coriander
2 tablespoons corn oil

Method

1. Peel shrimp. Prepare
   green mallow as
   described in step 2 of
   the recipe for Green
   Mallow with Poultry
   (page 149).

2. Boil water. Grate onion
   and season with salt
   and pepper. Rub onto
   shrimp.

3. Add onion, mastic
   grains, and shrimp to
   water. Boil for about
   10 minutes.

4. Add minced green
   mallow, and stir con-
   stantly for 5 minutes.
   Remove from heat.

5. Crush garlic and
   coriander. Fry in oil,
   then add to shrimp
   and mallow. Serve.

Shrimp Kufta with Rice

Ingredients

1 kilogram small white
   shrimp
1/2 cup finely blended rice
1 large onion
4 cloves garlic
1 bunch each parsley
   and mint
Salt and pepper
1 tablespoon cumin
1 egg, beaten
1/2 cup flour
Oil for deep frying
Parsley sprigs
Lime slices

Method

1. Wash and peel shrimp.

2. Sift rice and add to
   shrimp. Grind onion
   and garlic, finely chop
   parsley and mint, then
   mix all these ingredi-
   ents together.

3. Season mixture with
   salt, pepper, and
   cumin. Grind the whole
   mixture with a grinder.

4. Shape as desired into
   balls or fingers. Place
   in a vegetable steamer
   and steam for 10 min-
   utes over boiling water.

5. Coat shrimp kufta with
   egg, then with flour.
   Fry in hot oil. Serve on
   a plate, garnished with
   parsley and lime slices.

Oyster or Mussel Casserole
(Bram gandufli or Balah bahr)

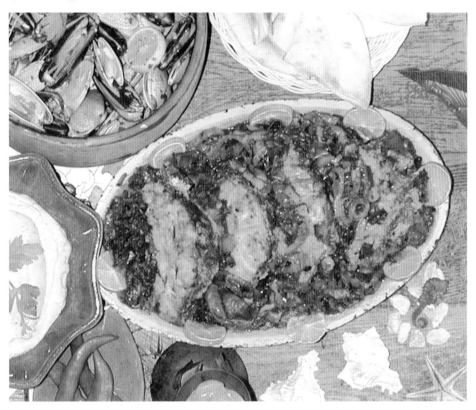

Ingredients

1 kilogram oysters or
mussels
4 cloves garlic
1 bunch parsley, chopped
Salt and pepper
1/8 kilogram butter
Juice of 2 limes

Method

1. Wash oysters or mussels well in running water to get rid of all the sand.

2. Finely chop garlic and parsley. Season with salt and pepper and mix with oysters or mussels. Place in an earthenware cooking vessel *(bram)*.

3. Add butter to top of *bram* in pieces, and bake in a medium hot oven for 30 minutes.

4. Add lime juice to bram immediately upon removing from oven. Serve hot.

Grilled Crab

Boiled Crab

Ingredients

Ingredients
1 kilogram crab (females)
1 large onion
1 tomato
1 lime
Salt and pepper
Lime slices

Method

1. Wash crab and place in a deep pot.

2. Slice onions, tomato, and lime. Season with salt and pepper and mix with crab.

3. Cook over medium heat for 15 minutes, shaking the pot occasionally to shift the crabs.

4. Arrange on a large serving dish and garnish with lime slices.

Ingredients

Ingredients
1 kilogram large crab
Salt and pepper
1 teaspoon cumin

Method

1. Wash crab and grill or bake in the oven for 15 minutes, flipping crab over from time to time.

2. Season the shell of the crab with salt, pepper, and cumin immediately upon removing from heat. Serve.

Note: Crabs must be eaten using hands and not with a fork and knife.

Sibia Casserole *(Tagin subayt)*

Ingredients
1 kilogram sibia
2 large onions
4 cloves garlic
1 bunch celery
1/2 kilogram tomatoes
1/4 cup corn oil
1 hot chili pepper
Salt and pepper
1 cup water
2 limes, sliced

Method

1. Wash sibia and sibia legs well. Cut sibia bodies into bite-sized pieces.

2. Slice onions and garlic. Chop celery and dice tomatoes.

3. Saute onion and garlic in oil until yellow. Add celery and chopped chili pepper then stir for 5 minutes. Add tomatoes seasoned with salt and pepper. Cook until sauce thickens and oil rises to the top.

4. Add 1 cup water to the mixture and bring to a boil. Add sibia. Pour whole mixture into an ovenproof dish. Garnish with lime slices and bake in a medium hot oven for 15 minutes until top is golden brown. Serve.

Fried Sibia *(Subayt maqli)*

Ingredients
1 kilogram large sibia or calamari
4 cloves garlic
Salt and pepper
1 tablespoon cumin
1 tablespoon prepared mustard
2 tablespoons oil
Juice of 2 limes
1 cup flour
Oil for deep frying
Lime slices

Method

1. Clean sibia bodies well by removing the bone, eyes, ink sack and the thin skin of the bodies. Cut into 2 cm thick strips. Soak in hot water for 10 minutes.

2. Crush garlic. Add salt, pepper, cumin, mustard, oil, and lime juice. Drain sibia and mix with above marinade and set aside 1 to 4 hours for flavors to develop.

3. Coat sibia in flour and deep fry in hot oil (about 5 cm deep). Arrange on serving plate and garnish with lime slices. Serve hot.

Seafood Rice

Ingredients

1/2 kilogram medium red shrimp

1/2 kilogram sibia

1/2 kilogram fish fillets (perch or bass)

Salt and pepper

1 onion

2 tablespoons corn oil

1 cup tomato juice

3 cups Fisherman's Style Rice (page 233)

1/4 kilogram hazelnuts

1/8 kilogram pine nuts

Method

1. Wash shrimp and peel. Wash sibia and cut into 1 cm thick slices. Wash fillets and season with salt and pepper.

2. Grate onion and fry lightly in oil until yellow in color. Add shrimp and squid and stir for a couple of minutes. Add tomato juice seasoned with salt and pepper. Cook until sauce thickens and oil rises to the top.

3. Mix above ingredients with prepared Fisherman's Style Rice.

4. Fry fish fillets in a little oil or butter. Peel skins, add to rice, then cook over low heat.

5. Boil hazelnuts for about 5 minutes, then cool. Peel, divide each nut in half and fry lightly in corn oil. Remove. Fry pine nuts lightly in oil and remove when a light golden color. Put the rice in a serving dish then garnish with pine nuts and serve.

Fried Silver-sided Fish *(Bisaria maqliya)*

Method

1. Wash fish well. Crush garlic, salt, pepper, and cumin. Mix with fish, then add lime juice.

2. Coat fish well in flour, then place in a colander to shake off any extra flour.

3. Heat oil well and deep fry fish until golden and crunchy. Silver-sided fish are eaten whole after removing only the heads.

Ingredients

Ingredients
1 kilogram silver-sided fish
4 cloves garlic
Salt and pepper
1 tablespoon cumin
1 tablespoon lime juice
1 cup flour
Oil for deep frying

Note: Silver-sided fish are tiny fish, smaller than a finger.

Silver-sided Fish Casserole *(Tagin bisaria)*

Ingredients

Ingredients
1 onion
2 tablespoons corn oil
2 cloves garlic
1 tablespoon cumin
1 cup tomato juice
Salt and pepper
1/2 cup water
1 kilogram silver-sided fish
1 tablespoon lime juice

Method

1. Chop onion and fry lightly in hot oil until yellow. Crush garlic with cumin and stir with onion for a couple of minutes. Add tomato juice and season with salt and pepper. Cook until sauce thickens and oil rises to the top.

2. Add water and bring to a boil. Add fish and cook over medium heat until fully cooked and sauce is thickened.

3. Add lime juice and serve.

Grains, Legumes, and Seeds

B ecause of their many nutritional and therapeutic benefits, grains, legumes, and seeds have sustained the health and life of many people for thousands of years. Today, grains and legumes form the staple diet of more than half the world's population.

Grains are the small, hard seeds of a food plant, such as wheat, rice, millet, corn, or oats. Legumes are the plants or pods or seeds of any plant of the legume family, characterized by herbaceous plants, shrubs, and vines with compound leaves and fruit in the form of pods, such as beans, peas, lentils, and peanuts. Due to the high cost of meats, we must depend on legumes as a main source of proteins, vitamins, minerals, and fibers, using them as an alternative to meat and poultry.

A large variety of dishes can be prepared using these valuable, and inexpensive, plant products.

Grains

Wheat

Wheat flour is an important source of vitamin B complex and is one of the richest natural sources of vitamin E. It also contains some vitamin D as well as important minerals such as calcium, magnesium, sodium, potassium, sulfur, zinc, iron, and copper.

Barley

The ancient Egyptians considered green barley to be a sexual stimulant due to its high vitamin content. It was also used to treat various illnesses and as a diuretic. Barley is a good food for children. Boiled and sprinkled with lime juice, it is one of the dietary treatments for diarrhea.

Maize

Kernels of maize, or corn, have been known to many of the world's peoples as a major food staple, and can be eaten in various forms: boiled, grilled, or popped as popcorn. Corn is also ground to make flour (cornmeal) which is used along with wheat flour to make bread and some desserts. Oil extracted from corn is widely used, as it is free from the saturated fats that clog the body's arteries, leading to cardiac diseases, cerebrovascular diseases, and hypertension.

Legumes

Legumes are an important food source for Egyptians and many of the most basic, traditional dishes are prepared with them.

Broad Beans (Fava Beans)
This legume is a very important staple food due to its high content of proteins and significant iron and minerals. When eaten green and fresh, broad beans supply good vitamins.

Chickpeas
Known since the times of the ancient Egyptians, chickpeas have been used either in their fresh form (malana) or dried. Chickpeas are rich in calcium and phosphorous and they contain small amounts of oxalic acid, which is a toxin. Excessive quantities of chickpeas should not be consumed, as they cause constipation. Chickpeas are believed to have a diuretic effect and to increase sexual desire and semen formation.

Lentils
Like other legumes, lentils are high in fiber and protein, and low in fat, but they have the added advantage of cooking quickly. Before cooking, always rinse and pick out stones and other debris left over from the harvesting process. Two kinds of lentils are used in Egyptian and most Middle-Eastern cooking—brown lentils, and the smaller orange split lentils. There is no need to soak lentils before cooking.

Seeds

Lupine
Egyptians have used lupines since ancient times both as food and as medication due to their high protein content, which forms 30 percent of their weight. Lupines also contain lecithin, which contains calcium and phosphorus, making them beneficial to good nerve and bone functions. They can also be used to cure deep wounds and skin rashes, as well as to ease intestinal pains.

Fenugreek
Known in Egypt since early times, fenugreek contains a mucoid substance as well as protein. Boiled fenugreek is recommended for the treatment of coughs, allergies, difficulties in breathing, and as

a mucolytic and expectorant. It is also a good antiflatulent and helps in cases of hemorrhoids. Fenugreek combats lethargy, and chest and liver diseases.

Recent studies that analyzed traditional foods such as stewed broad beans and falafil (bean cakes made from broad beans) strongly confirmed that these foods contain natural chemicals which impart feelings of happiness, calmness, and comfort. They do so by causing the brain to release a large number of neuropeptides with many different functions. They decrease anxiety, promote sleep, develop, and preserve memory. It was found that one cup stewed broad beans and two bean cakes, one of the most widely-consumed meals in Egypt, give all these benefits. Other legumes that were studied included lupines, stewed lentils, stewed white beans (great northern beans), chickpeas, and even white seeds *(lib abyad)*. These foods are best eaten with a source of vitamin C, such as lemons or limes, for the maximum benefit of 'happy hormones.'

It is better to soak dried vegetables before boiling to facilitate and shorten cooking. Legumes are first boiled for 10 minutes. The heat is then reduced, and they are left to simmer until fully cooked.

Note that dried legumes that have been stored for a long time require a longer soaking time, at least 10 hours.

If any worms or insects are found with the beans, discard the beans. Store beans in a dry, well- ventilated place, or keep them in the refrigerator to avoid infestation by worms and bugs.

The following are guidelines for required soaking and cooking times of various beans:

Type	Simmering time (after first 10 minutes of boiling)	Soaking time
blackeyed peas	at least 40 minutes	8 hours
white beans	at least 40 minutes	8 hours
stewed broad beans	at least 6 hours	8 hours
chickpeas	at least 4 hours	8 hours
whole wheat grains	at least 2 hours	8 hours

Bean Sprouts (*Ful nabit*)

Ingredients
1 kilogram dried white broad beans
Water

Method

1. Wash 1 kilogram of dried white broad beans. Cover with water and set aside for 24 hours. Water must be changed twice, but without moving the beans. This can be done by running the tap directly over the beans.

2. Strain water. Cover beans with a wet towel and allow 36 hours for the beans to sprout.

Broad Beans with Chard and Coriander (*Fuliyya*)

Ingredients
1 onion
2 tablespoons corn oil
2 bunches chard
1 liter water
1 kilogram broad beans
1/2 cup rice
Salt and pepper
4 cloves garlic
1 bunch fresh coriander

Method

1. Chop onion and fry lightly in oil until yellow.

2. Wash chard leaves. Chop chard stalks and rinse with water. Add to onion and stir until stalks turn yellow. Add water and bring to a boil.

3. Peel broad beans and add to water. Cook until the beans are nearly done, then add rice. Season with salt and pepper and continue cooking until fully cooked (about 30 minutes).

4. Boil chard leaves in a little bit of water and purée in blender. Add to previous mixture and continue cooking until mixture thickens. Serve in one large or several small deep dishes.

5. Crush garlic and chop fresh coriander. Fry in hot oil and sprinkle on top of bean dish. Serve.

Bean Sprout Stew *(Ful miqalli)*

Ingredients

2 onions
2 tablespoons corn oil
2 cups tomato juice
Salt and pepper
1 liter water
1 kilogram bean sprouts
1/2 cup rice
4 cloves garlic
1 tablespoon lime juice
1 bunch parsley, chopped

Method

1. Chop onions and saute lightly in oil until yellow in color.

2. Add tomato juice, season with salt and pepper and cook until sauce thickens and oil rises to the top.

3. Add water and bring to a boil. Peel bean sprouts by removing outer skin, then add and cook for 30 minutes.

4. Add rice and continue cooking until mixture thickens. Crush garlic and add to mixture. Boil for a few minutes, then add lime juice.

5. Serve in a deep dish, garnished with chopped parsley.

Bean Sprouts with Green Mallow

Ingredients

1 1/2 cups meat or
   chicken broth
1 onion
Salt and pepper
1 kilogram bean sprouts
1 kilogram fresh green
   mallow or 1 cup dried
   green mallow
   (mulukhiyya)
4 cloves garlic
2 tablespoons dried
   coriander
1 heaped tablespoon
   ghee

Method

1. Boil broth. Chop onion
   and season with salt
   and pepper. Add onion
   to broth and boil for a
   few minutes.

2. Add peeled bean
   sprouts (see previous
   recipe) and cook until
   well done (about 30
   minutes).

3. Add green mallow and
   stir for 5 minutes.

4. Crush garlic and
   coriander together. Fry
   in ghee, then add to
   green mallow. Boil for
   5 minutes. Serve.

Bean Sprout Kishk *(Kishk ful nabit)*

Ingredients

1 liter meat or chicken broth

4 cloves garlic, crushed

Salt and red pepper

1/2 kilogram bean sprouts

1 cup tomato juice

1/4 cup corn oil

Salt and pepper

1 cup yogurt

1/2 cup flour

1/2 cup water

1 large onion

Method

1. Boil broth. Add garlic, salt, and red pepper and boil for a few minutes.

2. Add bean sprouts after peeling. Cook until well done.

3. In another saucepan, place tomato juice, 1 tablespoon corn oil, salt, and pepper. Cook until sauce thickens and oil rises to the top.

4. Mix yogurt, flour, and water. Add to beans, stirring. Add cooked tomato sauce. Mix all ingredients and cook until it is thick.

5. Place in a deep dish. Slice onions and fry in remaining oil until golden brown. Use to garnish top of dish. Cool, then serve.

Crushed Beans Stewed with Greens *(Bisara khadra)*

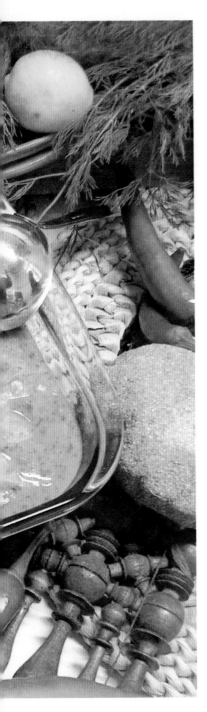

Ingredients

1/2 kilogram dried, crushed broad beans
1 bunch each parsley and coriander
Salt and red pepper
1 tablespoon cumin
1 tablespoon dried coriander
1 tablespoon caraway
2 tablespoons dried green mallow
1 tablespoon dried mint
4 cloves garlic
2 tablespoons corn oil
1 onion

Method

1. Wash beans with water several times until water runs clear. Place in a pot and cover with water. Add parsley and fresh coriander, chopped. Cook over low heat for 30 minutes without stirring.

2. Strain beans. Add salt, red pepper, cumin, coriander, and caraway. Cook, stirring constantly until mixture thickens. Add dried green mallow and mint.

3. Crush garlic and fry in 1 tablespoon oil. Add to mixture, cook for 5 more minutes, then pour onto small plates. Slice onion and fry in 1 tablespoon oil until golden. Garnish stewed beans with the fried onions and serve.

Crushed Beans Stewed with Bastirma
(Bisara safra bi-l-bastirma)

Ingredients

Same as previous recipe (page 201) but omit the greens (parsley, coriander, green mallow, mint), and use 1/4 kilogram *bastirma* without the outside crust (made up of crushed garlic, fenugreek and paprika) removed.

Method

1. Follow the same steps as the previous recipe.

2. Add 1/2 the amount of the *bastirma* to the beans after straining and during cooking in step 2, above.

3. Pour onto small plates and garnish with the remaining *bastirma* and fried onions. Serve.

Brown Lentils (*'Ads Abu Gibba*)

Ingredients

1/2 kilogram brown lentils
1 onion
2 tablespoons corn oil
1 cup tomato juice
Salt and pepper
1 liter water or broth
4 cloves garlic
2 tablespoons cumin
Green onions for
   serving

Method

1. Wash lentils. Soak for 1 hour, drain well, then place in a pot and cover with water. Simmer over low heat for 40 minutes until fully cooked. Rinse with cold water.

2. Chop onion and saute lightly in oil until yellow in color. Add tomato juice and season with salt and pepper. Cook until sauce thickens and oil rises to the top.

3. Add water or broth. Bring to a boil, then add boiled lentils.

4. Crush garlic and cumin. Add to mixture and boil for 5 minutes. Serve with green onions.

Brown Lentils with Rice and Macaroni
(*Kushari bi-li-'ads* or *Migadarra*)

Ingredients
2 large onions
Corn oil
1/2 cup vermicelli
Water
Salt
1 cup rice
1 cup brown lentils
1 cup small elbow macaroni
1/2 cup boiled chickpeas
Daqqa (tomato sauce):
6 cloves garlic
Salt and red pepper
1/4 cup corn oil
2 cups tomato juice
1/4 cup vinegar

Method

1. Slice onions and fry in oil in a deep pot. Remove onions and set aside. Fry vermicelli in the remaining hot oil until golden brown in color. Add 1 1/2 cups water and a little salt. Bring to a boil, add rice, and continue cooking until liquid is absorbed and rice is fully cooked.

2. Boil lentils in 2 cups water for 40 minutes over medium heat, then drain and rinse lentils with water. Place them in a pot with 1/4 cup water and heat over a low flame.

3. Bring a pot of water to a boil, add salt and a spoonful of oil, and boil macaroni until cooked. Rinse with cold water, then place in a pot with 1/4 cup water and a little salt and heat over a low flame.

4. To make *daqqa*: crush garlic, salt, and red pepper together. Fry in oil until a light golden brown. Add tomato juice and cook until sauce thickens and oil rises to the top. Add vinegar. Bring to boil.

5. To serve, layer components in the following order: rice with vermicelli followed by macaroni, then lentils, then chickpeas. Sprinkle fried onions on the top. Spoon *daqqa* over dish and serve.

Yellow Lentils with Rice *(Kushari asfar)*

Ingredients
1 tablespoon ghee
2 cups water
1 tablespoon salt
1 cup rice
1 cup yellow lentils

Method

1. Heat ghee. Add water and salt and bring to a boil.

2. Clean rice and lentils, by picking out any stones and other debris. Wash under running water, then add to boiling water.

3. Cook over medium heat, then over low heat until fully cooked. Serve with fried boiled eggs.

Note: You can garnish this dish with fried onions.

Lentil Soup with Rice or Vermicelli

Ingredients

3 cups lentil soup (see
recipe, page 37)
1/2 cup rice or vermicelli
4 cloves garlic
1/2 teaspoon cumin
1 tablespoon chopped
parsley

Method

1. Boil lentil soup and
add rice or vermicelli.
Cook until soup
thickens.

2. Crush garlic and
cumin and add to
mixture.

3. Serve in individual
dishes. Garnish with
parsley and serve.

Lentils with Chicken *('Ads abazi)*

Ingredients

1/2 kilogram yellow lentils
1 liter chicken broth
1 boiled chicken
1/4 kilogram cooked
ground meat
4 teaspoons crushed
garlic
1 onion
2 tablespoons ghee
1 tablespoon each cumin
and dried mint
1 bunch fresh coriander
Salt and pepper
1 tablespoon dried
coriander
1 bunch parsley, chopped
Salt and pepper

Method

1. Wash lentils and boil in
broth for 30 minutes
over low heat until the
mixture becomes thick.
Strain through a
vegetable strainer.

2. Remove bones from
boiled chicken. Cut
into small pieces and
arrange in an oven-
proof dish generously
coated with ghee.

3. Pour strained lentils
over chicken pieces.
Spoon ground meat on
lentils, then sprinkle 2
teaspoons of crushed
raw garlic over the dish.

4. Chop onion and fry in
ghee. Add to previous
mixture and season
with cumin, dried
mint, chopped fresh
coriander, and salt
and pepper.

5. Fry remaining garlic
and 1 tablespoon dried
coriander. Sprinkle
over above mixture
and garnish with
chopped parsley.

6. Bake in a medium hot
oven for 15 minutes
until top is browned.
Serve.

White Beans or Blackeyed Peas

Ingredients
1/2 kilogram white beans
1 onion
2 tablespoons ghee
1/2 kilogram meat, cubed
2 cups water
2 cups tomato juice
Salt and pepper
2 cups meat broth
2 cloves garlic, sliced

Method

1. Soak beans in cold water for 8 hours. Rinse. Cover with water and bring to a boil. Boil for 10 minutes, then lower heat and simmer for 30 minutes.

2. Chop onion and fry in ghee until yellow. Add cubed meat and stir meat and onion until all liquid is absorbed. Add water and continue cooking until meat is done.

3. Add tomato juice and season with salt and pepper. Cook until sauce thickens and ghee rises to the top.

4. Add broth and boil. Add boiled beans and garlic. Cook until sauce thickens and ghee rises to the top. Serve.

Note: You can make this recipe without the meat.

Cracked Wheat with Tail

(Firik bi-l-'akawi)

Ingredients

1/2 kilogram cracked wheat (firik)
1 kilogram tail bones and meat
1 onion
Salt and pepper
1 tablespoon ghee
1 tablespoon chopped parsley

Method

1. Soak cracked wheat in cold water for 8 hours.

2. Soak tail meat and bones in cold water for 1/2 hour.

3. Grate onion. Add salt and pepper. Strain meat and bones and put in a large pot. Add onion.

4. Drain cracked wheat and add to meat. Add ghee, cover with water and bring to a boil. Lower heat and simmer until fully cooked (about 1 hour).

5. Garnish with chopped parsley. Serve.

Stewed Broad Beans

(Ful midamis)

Method

1. Wash the beans, soak them in cold water for 8 hours, then drain.

2. Place in a dammasa, a special pot for stewing broad beans, or any large cooking pot. Cover with clean water and add 1/4 cup each of yellow lentils and whole wheat grains, one whole tomato and two whole cloves of garlic.

3. Bring to a boil and cook for 10 minutes.

Ingredients

1 kilogram of the beans called makmur or fava beans
1/4 cup yellow lentils
1/4 cup whole wheat grains
1 whole tomato
2 whole cloves garlic

4. Lower heat as much as possible and cook for 6–8 hours, adding 1 cup of boiling water and stirring when the beans are two-thirds of the way stewed.

Note: You may also use a weak electric heater for slow cooking.

Stewed Broad Beans with Oil and Lime Juice

Ingredients

1 cup stewed broad beans
2 tablespoons corn, olive, or linseed oil
1 teaspoon lime
1/2 teaspoon salt
1 teaspoon cumin
Pinch red pepper

Method

Season broad beans with oil, lime, and spices according to taste. Serve.

Broad Beans with Butter

Ingredients
1 teaspoon butter or ghee
1 cup stewed broad beans
Salt and pepper

Method

Place ghee or butter on serving plate. Heat beans, add to ghee, stir, and season with salt and pepper. Serve.

Broad Beans with Ghee and Garlic

Ingredients
2 cloves garlic
2 tablepoons ghee
1 cup stewed broad beans
Salt and pepper

Method

Slice garlic and fry lightly in ghee. Heat stewed beans, add garlic, and season with salt and pepper. Serve.

Broad Beans with Raw Garlic and Cumin

Ingredients
2 cloves garlic
1 tablespoon cumin
2 tablespoons corn oil
1 lime juice
1 red pepper
1 cup stewed broad beans

Method

1. Crush garlic and cumin together. Place in the bottom of a deep dish.

2. Add oil, lime juice, salt and red pepper. Heat broad beans, add to other ingredients, stir and serve.

Broad Beans with Tomatoes and Hot Chili Peppers

Ingredients

Ingredients
2 cloves garlic
2 tablespoons ghee
2 tomatoes
2 hot chili peppers
1 cup stewed broad beans
Salt and pepper

Method

1. Slice garlic and fry in ghee until yellow in color. Dice tomatoes and chili peppers, and add to ghee. Stir and cook until sauce thickens and ghee rises to the top.

2. Add stewed beans, salt, and pepper. Mix and serve.

Broad Beans with Eggs and Tomatoes

Ingredients
2 cloves garlic
2 tablespoons ghee
2 tomatoes
2 hot chili peppers
1 cup stewed broad beans
Salt and pepper

Method

1. Prepare beans in the same way as previous recipe.

2. Pour beans into an ovenproof dish. Using the back of a spoon, create 4 hollows and crack 1 egg into each hollow.

3. Cover dish and bake in a medium hot oven for 15 minutes. Remove cover and serve.

Broad Beans with Seasoning Mix

Ingredients

1 cup stewed broad beans
2 tablespoons corn oil
Juice of 2 limes
2 tablespoons tahini
Salt and red pepper
1 teaspoon cumin
1 tomato
1 hot chili pepper
2 cloves garlic

Method

1. Heat beans. Add oil, lime juice, tahini, salt, pepper, and cumin.

2. Dice tomato and chili pepper. Add to beans.

3. Mince garlic finely and add to mixture. Mash well with a fork, while cooking over very low heat. Serve as a sandwich filling for pita bread.

Strained Broad Beans *(Ful missafi)*

Ingredients

Ingredients
1 cup stewed broad beans
2 tablespoons corn oil
1 teaspoon lime juice
1/2 teaspoon cumin
Salt and red pepper

Method

1. Strain beans using a vegetable strainer to remove fibrous shells.

2. Season with oil, lime juice, cumin, salt, and red pepper. Heat over low flame. Serve.

Fried Crushed Bean
Patties *(Ta'miyya or Falafil)*

Ingredients

Ingredients
1 kilogram crushed broad beans
1 bunch parsley
1 bunch each fresh mint, coriander, and leeks
1/2 garlic head
1 large onion
Salt
1 tablespoon cumin
2 tablespoons dried coriander
1 teaspoon red pepper
1 egg
Sesame seeds
Oil for deep frying

Method

1. Soak crushed broad beans for 12 hours, then strain. Chop greens, garlic, and onion. Grind all ingredients well using an electric or manual grinder.

2. Season mix with salt, cumin, dried coriander, and red pepper. Refrigerate.

3. Beat egg and add to above mixture directly before frying. Shape into patties. Lightly dip each side in sesame seeds. Deep fry in hot oil (about 5 cm deep). Serve.

Note: Keep the mixture in several small bags in the freezer and use one each time.

Eggs

Eggs are a widely consumed food as they are a cheap source of animal protein and are very easily prepared. They are versatile, allowing the preparation of many different kinds of delicious dishes.

Nutritious meals for the whole family can be made with eggs, as they are high in protein and easy to digest , making them a breakfast favorite. Apart from protein, eggs are rich in iron, calcium, vitamins A, B, and D and good cholesterol, which the body needs to maintain vascular elasticity.

Recent studies have proven the benefit of egg consumption for all age groups, with no fear of vascular clogging. This is contrary to the widespread belief that eggs cause the accumulation of bad cholesterol in blood vessels, particularly in those aged 40 years and older. Due to the high nutrient value and easy digestibility of eggs, they are among the first foods given to infants after weaning, to supply their need of protein, vitamins, and iron (iron stores run out about 6 months after delivery). Eggs are one of the most important foods in child nutrition as they can be served directly, cooked in a variety of ways, or indirectly, as part of other foods such as cakes and desserts.

Hen eggs are the most commonly available eggs. Less common eggs are those of duck, goose, and quail. Goose eggs are the largest, and have a bluish tinge to the shell; duck eggs are slightly smaller. Quail eggs are quite small, and speckled.

Baladi eggs are smaller in size than farm hen eggs and have a distinct taste. They are characterized by the relatively large size of their yolk in comparison to the white. The yolk tends to be darker in color. *Baladi* eggs are better for boiling or frying purposes whereas farm eggs are better for making omelets.

Brown eggs tend to have a thicker shell, which makes them better for boiling as they don't easily crack. When the hens are fed both greens and grains, the yolk is darker in color.

Eggs must be stored in a cool place as soon as they are bought. They must not be kept longer than three weeks.

When boiling eggs, do not add them to boiling water just after taking them out of the refrigerator, but allow the eggs to sit at room temperature for a while to avoid cracks from the abrupt change in temperature.

When storing eggs in the refrigerator, they must be kept in a vertical position, with the wider part at the top. This maintains the circular shape of the yolk.

Fresh eggs are characterized by a circular yolk and a thick, clear, white. You can test your eggs for freshness by putting them in a bowl of salted water; fresh eggs sink to the bottom. When boiling eggs, it is advised to add two teaspoons of salt or some white vinegar. This prevents the white from seeping through the shell in case it does crack.

There are two ways to boil eggs:

In hot water, by placing the egg in already boiling water. A large egg requires:

12 minutes to hard-boil, 5–6 minutes to medium-boil, and 3–5 minutes to soft-boil.

In cold water, by placing the egg in cold water, then applying heat. A large egg requires:

10 minutes from the start of boiling to hard-boil. 4 minutes from the start of boiling to medium-boil, and 3 minutes from the start of boiling to soft-boil.

Eggs must be rinsed in cool water as soon as they reach the desired doneness. If boiled eggs are left in the boiling water, the yolk turns a grayish color.

Eggs are better eaten as soon as they are cooked, or within a maximum of 2 days after refrigerating. Some people prefer to season boiled eggs with *duqqa* and not just salt and pepper.

There are Two Types of *Duqqa*

Regular *duqqa*: a mixture of salt, cumin, and sesame seeds, all ground together.

***Duqqa* with thyme,** which is made from the following ingredients:

1 tablespoon cumin

1 tablespoon dried coriander

1 cup sesame seeds

1 cup shelled local (small) dried chickpeas, soaked in hot water for 1 hour

2 tablespoons thyme

1 tablespoon salt

1/4 cup black cumin

Method

1. Toast cumin, dried coriander, and 1/2 cup sesame seeds.

2. Add above mix to chickpeas, thyme, and salt. Finely grind in clean coffee grinder.

3. Toast remaining 1/2 cup sesame seeds and black cumin. Add to above mixture without grinding.

4. Store in a clean, tightly sealed jar. Serve with eggs.

Omelet

Ingredients
2 large eggs
Salt and pepper
1/4 teaspoon cumin
1 tablespoon ghee or corn oil

Method

1. Beat eggs and season with salt, pepper, and cumin.

2. Heat oil or ghee. Add eggs and cook until set.

3. Flip onto other side. Cook until golden brown. Serve.

Egyptian Omelet (ʿIgga)

Ingredients
1 onion
1/4 cup corn oil
6 eggs
Salt and pepper
2 tablespoons flour
2 tablespoons chopped parsley

Method

1. Chop onion and saute in oil until yellow in color.

2. Beat eggs and season with salt and pepper. Add flour, parsley, and sauteed onion. Beat with a whisk or a fork.

3. Heat oil. Add egg mixture and cook until set. Flip over and cook until golden brown. Serve.

Omelet with Vegetables and Cheese
(ʿIgga bi-l-khudar wi-l-gibna)

Ingredients
2 tomatoes
1 sweet pepper
2 heaped tablespoons grated sharp cheese (such as rumi, parmesan, romano)
1/4 cup oil

Method

1. Follow steps 1 and 2 of previous recipe (page 224).

2. Dice tomatoes and pepper. Add to above mixture along with grated cheese.

3. Add oil to a Teflon baking pan and add egg mixture. Bake in a medium hot oven for 15 minutes until fully cooked and top is lightly browned. Serve.

Baked Eggs with Tomato Mixture
(Shakshuka)

Ingredients
1 large onion
2 cloves garlic
2 tablespoons ghee
1/2 kilogram tomatoes
2 hot chili peppers
1/2 cup water
Salt and pepper
6 eggs
1 tablespoon chopped parsley

Method

1. Slice onion and garlic and saute lightly in ghee until yellow in color.

2. Dice tomatoes and chili peppers. Add, stirring until tomatoes are half cooked. Add water, salt, and pepper.

3. Pour mixture into a Teflon pan. Using the back of a spoon, make six hollows and crack one egg into each.

4. Bake in a medium hot oven for 15 minutes. Garnish top with chopped parsley. Serve.

Scrambled Eggs with Butter

Ingredients
1 tablespoon butter
2 eggs
Salt and pepper

Method

1. Heat butter in a skillet. Add eggs and stir rapidly to mix whites, yolks and butter. Cook until set.

2. Season with salt and pepper and serve immediately.

Rice and Egg Broth *(Sakhina)*

Ingredients

1 onion

2 tablespoons corn oil

1/2 liter water

Salt and pepper

1 tablespoon cumin

1 tablespoon caraway
  seeds

1/2 cup rice

6 eggs

Method

1. Chop onion and saute lightly in oil until yellow.

2. Add 2 cups water and season with salt, pepper, cumin, and caraway. Bring to a boil.

3. Wash rice and add to boiling water, simmering for about 10 minutes until almost cooked.

4. Crack eggs, one by one into mixture, and cook for 5 minutes.

5. Serve as a soup with poached eggs.

Eggs with Rice

Ingredients
1 onion
2 tablespoons ghee
2 cups chicken broth
or water
Salt and pepper
2 cups rice
4 eggs

Method

1. In sauce pan, chop onion and saute lightly in ghee until golden yellow in color.

2. Add broth and season with salt and pepper. Bring to a boil.

3. Add rice and cook until liquid is almost absorbed. Make 4 hollows in the rice and crack one egg into each, leaving equal spaces between each hollow.

4. Cover saucepan and cook over low heat until fully cooked. Serve.

Boiled Fried Eggs
(Bayd miza'lil)

Method

1. Hard boil eggs (10 minutes).

2. Peel eggs, season with salt and pepper, and fry in ghee until golden brown. Serve.

Ingredients
4 eggs
Salt and pepper
2 teaspoons ghee

Note: Boiled fried eggs are always served next to yellow lentils with rice or brown lentils with rice and pasta to increase their nutritional value.

227

Eggs with Cooked Ground Meat

Ingredients

1 onion
2 tablespoons ghee
1/4 kilogram ground meat
1/4 cup water
Salt and pepper
4 eggs

Method

1. Chop onion and saute lightly in ghee until yellow. Add meat, stir and cook.

2. When almost cooked, add water, salt, and pepper. Continue cooking until all liquid is absorbed and meat is browned.

3. Make 4 hollows in the mixture with the back of a spoon and crack one egg into each. Cover and cook for 5 minutes or until eggs are done.

4. Sprinkle with a little pepper. Serve.

Eggs with Pitted Dates

Ingredients

2 tablespoons flour
2 tablespoons ghee
1/4 kilogram pitted, chopped dates
4 eggs

Method

1. Fry flour in ghee until color turns yellow. Add dates and stir, mashing to form a soft pulp.

2. Crack eggs into mixture stirring and cooking until eggs are set. Serve hot.

Eggs with Bastirma Sausage (Suguq) and Tomato

Ingredients

1/4 kilogram *suguq* (sausage)
1/4 kilogram *bastirma* without outer crust
2 teaspoons ghee
1/4 kilogram tomatoes
1 hot chili pepper
Salt and pepper
4 eggs

Method

1. Chop *suguq* into bite-sized pieces. Add to *bastirma* and stir for a few minutes in ghee.

2. Dice tomatoes and chili pepper. Add to above mix and season with salt and pepper. Cook until tomatoes are stewed.

3. Make 4 hollows in the mixture with the back of a spoon and crack one egg into each. Cover and cook for 5 minutes. Serve.

Rice, Fatta, and Pasta

R ice is a staple of Egyptian meals and is often served alongside cooked vegetables. Egyptians commonly eat rice cooked on its own, as a side dish with fish and other meals, or combined with macaroni and brown lentils to make the well-known Egyptian dish, *kushari* (see page 205). Egyptian rice dishes include rice with vermicelli, rice with fried rice, and fisherman's style rice, while the combination of rice and bread to form fatta is also a typically Egyptian meal. Fried vermicelli, whether savory or sweet, with fried nuts can make a complete meal, as can pasta with meat, onions, tomato, and garlic for a savory lunch. Couscous is a well-known Moroccan dish that is also served in Egypt, with the added touch of sugar and fried nuts.

Plain Rice
(Urz mifalfil)

Ingredients

1 tablespoon ghee
2 cups water
1 teaspoon salt
2 cups rice

Method

1. Heat ghee. Add water and salt and bring to a boil.

2. Clean and wash rice. Add to boiling water. Cook until water is almost absorbed, then lower heat, and continue cooking for about 10 minutes. Serve.

Rice with Vermicelli

Ingredients

1/2 cup vermicelli
1 tablespoon ghee
2 1/2 cups water
1 tablespoon salt
2 cups rice

Method

1. Break vermicelli into small pieces. Fry in ghee until golden. Add water and salt and bring to a boil.

2. Wash rice and add to boiling water. Cook uncovered until liquid is almost absorbed.

3. Stir rice, cover and continue cooking over low heat until fully cooked. Serve.

Rice with Fried Rice *(Urz habba wi habba)*

Ingredients
2 cups rice
1 tablespoon ghee
2 cups water
1 teaspoon salt

Method

1. Fry 1/2 cup rice in ghee until brown. Add water and salt and bring to a boil.

2. Add remaining rice and stir. Cook covered until liquid is almost absorbed. Lower heat and continue cooking until rice is well done. Serve.

Rice with Tomato Juice

Method

1. Melt ghee. Add tomato juice and cook until sauce thickens and ghee rises to the top.

2. Add water, salt, and pepper and bring to a boil.

3. Add chickpeas and boil for 5 minutes. Add rice, cover, and cook until liquid is absorbed.

Ingredients
1 tablespoon ghee
1 cup tomato juice
2 1/2 cups water
Salt and pepper
1/4 cup small dried chickpeas, soaked in hot water for 1 hour
2 cups rice

4. Stir rice and lower heat. Cook until well done, about 20 minutes. Serve.

Fisherman's Style Rice/Fish Rice
(Urz sayadiyya)

Ingredients
1 large onion
2 tablespoons corn oil
1 tablespoon tomato paste
2 1/2 cups water
1 teaspoon cumin
1/4 teaspoon cinnamon
1/4 teaspoon nutmeg
Salt and pepper
2 cups rice

Method

1. Chop onion and fry in oil until a dark brown color.

2. Add tomato paste and stir. Add a little water to dissolve the onion and tomato paste.

3. Add the rest of the water and the spices. Bring to a boil.

4. Wash rice and add to boiling water. Cover and cook until liquid is almost absorbed.

5. Stir, lower heat, and continue cooking for 20 minutes or until well done. Serve.

White Rice with Chopped Chicken Liver and Gizzards

Ingredients

1/4 kilogram chicken liver
and gizzard
Salt and pepper
2 tablespoons ghee
2 cups rice
2 cups broth

Method

1. Chop liver and gizzards into small pieces. Season with salt and pepper and fry in 1 tablespoon ghee. Lower heat and continue cooking until well done.

2. In another saucepan, melt 1 tablespoon ghee. Add rice and stir until rice becomes yellow.

3. Add broth and bring to a boil. Add salt. Cover and cook until liquid is almost absorbed. Lower heat and continue cooking until well done.

4. Spoon rice onto a large serving dish and arrange fried liver and gizzard pieces on the top as garnish.

Rice with Peas, Carrots, and Béchamel

Ingredients

1/4 kilogram peas, shelled

2 carrots, diced

2 cups cooked plain rice

Béchamel sauce:

2 tablespoons ghee

2 cups milk

Salt and pepper

1 egg

Method

1. Saute peas and carrots.

2. Make béchamel: Fry flour in 1 tablespoon ghee until color turns yellow. Add milk, stirring constantly until mixture thickens. Season with salt and pepper. Cool.

3. Mix rice with peas and carrots. Add 2 tablespoons béchamel sauce and mix.

4. Grease an ovenproof dish with 1 tablespoon ghee. Spoon some béchamel sauce on the bottom. Add rice mixed with vegetables, then cover with remaining béchamel sauce.

5. Beat egg and season with pepper. Brush onto béchamel top.

6. Bake in a medium hot oven for 15 minutes or until top is lightly browned. Serve.

Note: You may add a little cooked ground beef to the rice and vegetables, if desired.

235

Khalta Rice with Nuts and Chicken Livers *(Urz bi-l-khalta)*

Ingredients

2 cups rice

1 tablespoon sugar

1 tablespoon water

2 tablespoons ghee

2 cups chicken broth

Salt and pepper

Bay leaf

1 cinnamon stick

1/4 kilogram chicken livers

2 tablespoons ghee

1/4 cup raisins

2 tablespoons pine nuts

1/4 cup almonds, boiled
  and peeled

Method

1. Wash rice and set aside in a sieve to dry.

2. Place sugar and water in a pot over medium heat. Cook until sugar becomes a dark brown color. Add 2 tablespoons ghee and stir, then add rice and stir.

3. Cook rice over low heat, stirring occasionally until rice is light brown in color.

4. Add broth, salt, and pepper. Bring to a boil, then add bay leaf and cinnamon stick.

5. When liquid is almost absorbed, lower heat, cover, and continue cooking until rice is fully cooked.

6. Chop chicken livers into small pieces and fry in a little ghee. Season with salt and pepper and cook over low heat until fully cooked and browned. Remove.

7. Fry raisins in remaining ghee until puffed, then remove. Lightly fry pine nuts until golden, then remove.

8. Split almonds in half. Fry lightly in ghee, then remove.

9. Spoon rice onto a large round serving plate. Garnish with fried liver and nuts. Serve. (Remember to remove bay leaf and cinnamon stick before serving).

Note: *Khalta* rice is served with chicken, duck, or stuffed pigeon. Chickens and ducks are quartered and arranged around the rice. Pigeons are served whole.

Fatta with Milk and Yogurt

Ingredients
2 loaves of stale baladi bread
1 tablespoon ghee
Salt and pepper
2 cups meat broth
4 cloves garlic
1 teaspoon salt
1 cup yogurt
1 kilogram boiled meat

Method

1. Cut bread into small squares and fry in a little ghee. Sprinkle with salt and pepper, then soak with broth.

2. Crush garlic and salt and mix with yogurt. Cover top of bread mixture with the yogurt. Place in a medium hot oven for 5 minutes.

3. Arrange boiled meat pieces around the plate and serve.

Meat Fatta (*Fattat al-lahm*)

Ingredients
1 kilogram meat (shin or neck)
2 loaves of stale baladi bread
Salt and pepper
2 tablespoons ghee
4 cloves garlic
2 tablespoons vinegar
2 cups cooked plain rice

Method

1. Cook meat by boiling in water to make broth.

2. Cut bread into small pieces and season with salt and pepper. Coat with 1 tablespoon ghee and place in a low oven until golden brown and crisp. Arrange in a serving dish.

3. Pour about 1 cup meat broth over bread and set aside until broth is absorbed.

4. Crush garlic and fry in 1 tablespoon ghee until yellow in color. Add vinegar and 1/2 cup broth and bring to a boil.

5. Add some of the above sauce to the bread, then cover with rice. Add the remaining vinegar sauce to the rice and sprinkle with pepper.

6. To serve, place the boiled meat and soup in one bowl and the *fatta* (rice and bread) in another serving dish. Another way of serving *fatta* is to fry the boiled meat pieces in a spoon of ghee, and arrange them around the rice with the broth in a separate bowl.

Shanks Fatta *(Fattat al-kawari')*

Ingredients
Same as recipe opposite, but replace meat with beef shanks

Method

1. Boil shanks to prepare shank broth (page 35).

2. Follow the same steps, but remove meat from bones and arrange on top of *fatta*. Serve.

239

Lentil Fatta *(Fattat al-'ads)*

Ingredients

2 loaves of stale baladi
 bread
2 tablespoons ghee
2 cups lentil soup (see
 recipe, page 37)
4 cloves garlic
2 tablespoons vinegar
Pepper

Method

1. Cut bread in small squares, coat in 1 tablespoon ghee and toast. Pour hot lentil soup over bread and set aside until absorbed.

2. Chop garlic and fry in 1 tablespoon ghee until yellow. Add vinegar. Sprinkle on top of fatta along with some pepper. Serve.

Green Mallow Fatta *(Fattat al-mulukhiyya)*

Ingredients

2 loaves of stale baladi
 bread
2 tablespoons ghee
Pepper
2 cups dried or green
 mallow (*mulukhiyya*, see
 recipe, page 49), cooked

Method

1. Cut bread into small squares, coat with ghee, sprinkle with pepper and toast for a few minutes in the oven.

2. Add cooked *mulukhiyya* to bread and set aside for 5 minutes until bread is moistened. Serve with meat or poultry.

Bean Sprout Fatta *(Fattat al-ful al-nabit)*

Ingredients

1/2 kilogram bean sprouts
2 loaves of stale baladi bread
1 tablespoon ghee
1 large onion
2 tomatoes
2 tablespoons corn oil
Juice of 2 limes
Salt and pepper

Method

1. Peel bean sprouts by removing outer skin, and boil (see page 37). Reserve 1 cup of the cooking broth.

2. Cut bread in small squares and fry in ghee. Place in a deep bowl and add 1 cup bean sprout broth. Set aside until liquid is absorbed.

3. Dice onion and tomatoes. Cover bread with bean sprouts, then with onions and tomatoes.

4. Mix oil, lime juice, salt, and pepper and pour over *fatta*. Serve.

Spaghetti with Tomato Sauce

Ingredients

1/2 kilogram spaghetti
(or any desired pasta)
1 1/2 liters water
1 teaspoon salt
1 tablespoon oil
1 onion
2 tablespoons ghee
1/4 kilogram ground beef
1/4 cup water
1 cup tomato juice
Salt and pepper

Method

1. Boil pasta in water. Add salt and oil. Cook for 20 minutes, then drain and rinse with cold water.

2. Chop onion and saute in ghee until yellow in color. Add ground meat and stir until juices are absorbed and meat is browned. Add water and cook until liquid is absorbed.

3. Add tomato juice and season with salt and pepper. Cook until sauce thickens and ghee rises to the top.

4. Rinse pasta with hot water and serve. Serve ground meat in tomato sauce in a separate dish to be added according to taste.

Pasta with Onion and Meat Cubes

Ingredients
2 onions
4 cloves garlic
Salt and pepper
1 teaspoon mixed spice
1/2 kilogram lamb meat,
cut into small cubes
2 cups tomato juice
2 tablespoons ghee
2 cups meat broth
1/2 kilogram elbow pasta
(or any small pasta)

Method

1. Slice onions and garlic. Season with salt, pepper, and mixed spice.

2. Add meat cubes, tomato juice, and ghee. Cook over medium heat until fully cooked.

3. Add meat broth and bring to a boil.

4. Add pasta and cook until liquid is almost completely absorbed. Continue cooking over low heat or bake in a medium hot oven, for 15 minutes. Serve.

243

Rosamarina Casserole

Ingredients
Same as for Spaghetti with Tomato Sauce (page 242) but use rosamarina pasta instead of spaghetti.

Method

1. Boil pasta. Prepare tomato sauce as previously described on page 242. Mix together.

2. Grease an ovenproof dish with a little ghee. Add pasta and tomato sauce, reserving ground meat from sauce. Sprinkle top of casserole with reserved ground beef.

3. Bake in a medium hot oven for 15 minutes until top is lightly browned. Serve.

Pasta with Béchamel Sauce

Ingredients

1/2 kilogram penne pasta
1/4 kilogram cooked
    ground beef
1 egg
Salt and pepper

Béchamel sauce:
2 tablespoons flour
2 tablespoons ghee
4 cups milk
1 teaspoon salt

Method

1. Cook pasta as usual and rinse with cold water.

2. Prepare béchamel sauce: fry flour in ghee until it becomes yellow in color. Add cold milk, stirring constantly until mixture thickens. Add salt and cool.

3. Pour a little of the béchamel sauce in an ovenproof dish. Add half the pasta, cover with ground meat, then add the remaining pasta. Cover top with béchamel sauce.

4. Beat egg with fork, and add a little salt and pepper. Brush onto top of béchamel.

5. Bake in a hot oven for about 1 hour until top is golden brown. Serve.

Note: You may add two spoons of tomato paste to cooked ground beef if desired.

Fried Vermicelli

Ingredients

1/2 kilogram vermicelli
    pasta
1 tablespoon ghee
2 cups water

Method

1. Break pasta into small
   pieces and fry in ghee
   until golden brown in
   color. Add water and
   bring to a boil.

2. When liquid is almost
   absorbed, lower heat,
   and continue cooking
   until done. Serve.

Vermicelli with Khalta Mix

Method

1. Prepare vermicelli as described opposite. Season with salt and pepper.

2. Prepare liver pieces and nuts in the same way as for *Khalta* Rice (see recipe, page 143). Use to garnish top of vermicelli. Serve.

Vermicelli with Sugar

Method

1. Prepare fried vermicelli as described opposite.

2. Serve hot along with a dish of powdered sugar and another dish of toasted almonds, raisins, and pine nuts which are to be added to taste.

248

Couscous

Ingredients

Ingredients
2 kilograms white or semolina flour
1/2 teaspoon salt
2 cups water

Method

1. Sift flour and salt. Sprinkle lightly with water until evenly moistened.

2. Rub between the palms of both hands to form short strings.

3. Force through a wide-holed colander to form large, round grains.

4. Using a couscous pot, steam for 30 minutes. Cool. Sprinkle once more with water.

5. Force through a narrow-holed colander to form fine, round grains. Steam for a further 10 minutes.

6. Add ghee to hot couscous and stir well.

7. Serve couscous as a savory dish with kufta (see recipe for rice kufta on page 132), or serve as a dessert with pow-dered sugar, toasted nuts, and hot milk.

Pastry

Traditional Egyptian pastry derives from the particular method of kneading wheat flour, water, and a little salt to form different types of pastries, which define Egyptian cuisine. Nowadays, you can find many different types of ready-made doughs, such as filo dough, *ruqaq*, *qata'if*, and so on. There are special shops in Egypt for these ingredients, but they can also be found in most supermarkets.

The most famous of Egyptian pastries is *fitir mishaltit* (Egyptian pancake), which requires its dough to be stretched and folded over many times, each time coated generously with ghee, to produce thin layers of the delicious *fitir* which is baked and can be eaten with mature cheese or with honey.

Ruqaq

Ingredients

1 liter chicken or meat
  broth
1/2 cup milk
Salt and pepper
1/4 cup ghee
1 kilogram *ruqaq*

For *mu'sag*:
1/2 kilogram ground beef
2 large onions
1 table spoon ghee
1 cup water

Method

1. Chop onion and sauté in ghee until yellow in color. Add ground meat and stir until juices are absorbed and meat is browned. Add water and cook until liquid is absorbed.

2. Boil broth. Add milk, salt, pepper, and 2 tablespoons ghee.

3. Melt the remaining ghee and coat the base of a rectangular oven pan. Wet sheets of *ruqaq* in broth mixture and arrange in layers, sprinkling some melted ghee between each layer.

4. After layering half the *ruqaq*, spread ground meat on top. Add the remaining *ruqaq* in the same manner.

5. Sprinkle some ghee on the top. Bake in a medium hot oven for 30 minutes until top is lightly browned. Cut into squares and serve.

Note: *Ruqaq* is a cracker-like bread.

Gulash with Cheese and Eggs

Ingredients

1/2 kilogram gulash
  filo dough)
1/2 cup ghee
1/4 kilogram grated *rumi*
  cheese (or other sharp
  cheese)
2 eggs
2 cups milk
Salt and pepper

Method

1. Grease the bottom of a large rectangular oven pan (29 x 39 cm). Arrange half the gulash sheets, sprinkling some melted ghee every other layer.

2. Spread grated cheese. As a variation, add cooked ground meat alone or with cheese or puréed spinach. Spread remaining gulash sheets in the same manner. Sprinkle top with ghee and bake in a medium hot oven for 15 minutes.

3. Beat eggs and milk. Season with a little pepper. Remove pan from oven and cut gulash into squares. Pour milk and egg mixture over gulash and bake for a further 15 minutes until top is golden brown. Serve.

Gulash Fingers with Ground Beef

Ingredients

1/2 kilogram gulash
(filo dough)
4 tablespoons ghee
1/4 kilogram cooked
ground beef
1/8 kilogram grated *rumi*
cheese (or other sharp
cheese)

Method

1. Cut gulash sheets into
rectangles. Grease
each rectangle lightly
with ghee.

2. Place 1 teaspoon meat
and 1/2 teaspoon
cheese at the end of
each rectangle and roll
into individual fingers,
closing the sides while
rolling. Continue doing
this until you run out of
ingredients.

3. Brush top of gulash
fingers with ghee and
arrange in an oven pan.
Bake in a medium hot
oven for 15 minutes
until top is lightly
browned. Serve.

Qata'if with Meat and Cheese Filling
(Qata'if bi-l-'assag wi-l-gibna)

Ingredients

1/4 kilogram cooked
   ground beef
2 tablespoons grated *rumi*
   cheese (or other sharp
   cheese)
2 tablespoons chopped
   parsley
1/2 kilogram *qata'if* (small
   round pastry resem-
   bling pancakes)
Oil for deep frying

Method

1. Mix meat, cheese,
   and chopped parsley.

2. Place filling in center
   of each *qata'if*, fold
   qata'if in half over
   filling, and press on
   sides firmly all around
   to close.

3. Deep fry in hot oil
   (about 5 cm deep)
   until golden brown.

4. Remove from oil and
   serve on a plate,
   garnished with parsley.

Note: You can substitute meat
and *rumi* cheese filling with
white soft cheese, adding
dried mint, and some pitted
olive halves.

Egyptian Pancakes *(Fitir mishaltit)*

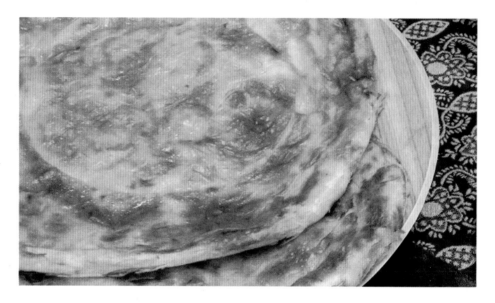

Ingredients
2 cups flour
1/2 cup water
1/2 teaspoon salt
1/4 cup ghee

Method

1. Sift flour. Make a well in the middle and add water and salt. Mix dough, kneading well and stretching the dough several times for about 10 minutes. Set aside 30 minutes to rest.

2. Using a rolling pin, spread out dough in the shape of a large circle. Pull at edges all around, gently so as not to tear the dough.

3. Generously coat the whole circle of dough with ghee. Fold over from all sides about 6 times coating with ghee each time. Shape the dough into a circle, about 30 cm in diameter.

4. Place the *fitir* in an oven pan (30 cm) greased with ghee. Bake in a medium hot oven for about 30 minutes until golden brown. Brush water on top as soon as it is brought out of the oven. Serve with honey and cream or with *falahi* white cheese or *mish*.

Turnovers *(Sambusik)*

Ingredients

3 cups flour

1/2 teaspoon salt

2 tablespoons ghee

2 tablespoons corn oil

3 eggs

1 cup warm water

Oil for deep frying

Filling:

1/4 kilogram cooked
   ground beef or 1/4
   kilogram low salt white
   cheese

1 tablespoon dried mint

Method

1. Sift flour. Add salt, ghee, and oil. Mix with fingertips until flour absorbs fats.

2. Beat eggs and add to above mixture. Add water and mix well. Knead dough until it becomes firm and easy to spread.

3. Divide dough into lime-sized pieces, then rest for about 1 hour.

4. Roll out individual pieces to form long, thin rectangles.

5. Combine filling ingredients. Place filling on the edge of the dough. Fold over several times to close in triangular shapes.

6. Deep fry in hot oil (about 5 cm deep). Serve hot.

Meat-stuffed Dough
(Hawawshi)

Method

1. Dissolve yeast and 1 teaspoon sugar in 1 cup warm water. Add a little of the flour. Mix and set aside in a warm place for 15 minutes until dough rises.

2. Sift flour. Add salt, sugar, oil, and 2 eggs. Mix with fingertips until absorbed.

3. Add yeast to above mixture. Knead well. Set aside in a warm place for 1 hour, until dough rises.

4. Divide dough into 6 balls. Roll each into a circle (about 1 cm thick).

5. Make filling: combine meat, onions, parsley, and chili pepper. Season with salt, pepper, and mixed spice. Stuff dough rounds with this mixture. Fold dough in half, pressing the edges closed firmly with fingers.

6. Brush tops with 1 beaten egg. Sprinkle with sesame and black cumin seeds Set aside to rise for 30 minutes.

7. Bake in a hot oven for 30 minutes until tops are highly browned. Serve.

Ingredients

1 packet dry yeast (10 g)
1 teaspoon sugar
1 cup warm water
3 cups flour
Pinch of salt
2 tablespoons sugar
1/3 cup corn oil
3 eggs
Sesame seeds
Black cumin seeds (habit al-baraka)

Filling:
1 kilogram ground beef
2 large onions, chopped
2 tablespoons parsley, chopped
1 hot chili pepper, chopped
Salt and pepper
2 tablespoons mixed spice

259

Pastry Stuffed with Meat and Vegetables

Ingredients

Same ingredients as for
   turnovers (see page
   257)
2 tablespoons ghee, to
   brush on pastry

Filling:
1/4 kilogram cooked
   ground beef
1 cup boiled peas
1 cup boiled diced carrots

Method

1. Prepare dough as
   previously described
   on page 257. Roll out
   dough in the shape of
   squares and coat with
   a layer of ghee.

2. Combine filling
   ingredients. Place
   1 tablespoon filling in
   the center of each
   square. Fold each
   corner inwards to
   form a smaller square.

3. Brush top of each
   pastry with ghee and
   arrange in a large oven
   pan. Bake in a hot
   oven until fully cooked
   and golden in color.
   Remove from oven.

4. Brush tops with water
   immediately after
   removing from oven
   to get the desired rose
   color. Serve.

Salads

S alads of raw and cooked vegetables are a vital part of any main meal in Egypt and not merely a side dish. In Egypt, fresh vegetables were traditionally sold by street vendors, whereas today they are available in grocery shops and supermarkets as well. Particular combinations of vegetables and spices make uniquely Egyptian salads, with eggplants a favorite ingredient, served either with garlic or with tomato sauce and vinegar.

Vegetables such as leek, green onions, and water cress are the natural companion to cheese, beans, and falafel for most of Egypt's people. Always wash and dry vegetables thoroughly before cooking or cutting them.

Green Salad

Ingredients
2 cucumbers
Lettuce
1 hot chili pepper
2 tomatoes
1 carrot
Salad dressing:
Salt and pepper
1 teaspoon lime juice
1 teaspoon corn oil
1 tablespoon vinegar

Method

1. Wash and dry vegetables well. Cut all (except carrot) into large pieces and mix in a salad bowl. Grate carrot and use to garnish top of the salad.

2. Prepare the dressing by mixing all the ingredients together with a fork. Add to salad immediately before serving.

263

Local Salad *(Salata baladi)*

Ingredients
1 bunch watercress
2 firm tomatoes
2 cucumbers
1 large onion
Salad dressing (as on page 262)

Method

1. Wash and dry vegetables well. Dice all (except onion) into small pieces and mix in a deep dish.

2. Dice onion and use to garnish top of the salad.

3. Prepare dressing and add to salad. Serve immediately.

Tomato Slices

Ingredients
2 large firm tomatoes
2 cloves garlic, finely sliced
1 tablespoon corn oil
Juice of 1 lime
Salt and pepper
1/2 teaspoon cumin

Method

1. Slice tomatoes and arrange in a serving dish. Garnish with garlic.

2. Season with oil, lime juice, salt, pepper, and cumin. Serve.

Tomatoes with Onions

Ingredients
2 firm tomatoes
1 large onion
1 tablespoon chopped parsley
Salad dressing (as on page 262)

Method

1. Dice tomatoes and onions and mix. Garnish with parsley.

2. Add salad dressing and serve.

Potato Salad

Ingredients
2 boiled potatoes
2 cloves garlic
2 tablespoons corn oil
1 teaspoon lime juice
Salt and pepper
1/2 teaspoon cumin
2 tablespoons chopped parsley

Method

1. Cube potatoes. Crush garlic and mix with oil, lime juice, salt, pepper, and cumin. Mix with potatoes.

2. Garnish with parsley and serve.

Beetroot Salad

Ingredients
1/2 kilogram beetroots, boiled
Salad dressing (as on page 262)
2 tablespoons chopped parsley

Method

Peel and cube beets and combine with dressing. Garnish with parsley and serve.

Stuffed Tomatoes

Ingredients

4 small tomatoes

4 cloves garlic

Salt and pepper

1 tablespoon cumin

1 tablespoon coriander

1 hot chili pepper

1 tablespoon lime juice

1 tablespoon corn oil

Method

1. Make a horizontal slice through the upper part of each tomato to remove the cap. Make two incomplete vertical cuts to divide into quarters.

2. Crush garlic, salt, pepper, cumin, coriander, and hot chili pepper. Add lime juice. Use mix to stuff tomatoes. Sprinkle with oil and serve.

White Bean Salad

Ingredients

1/4 kilogram white beans

2 cloves garlic

Salt and pepper

1 teaspoon cumin

1 teaspoon lime juice

2 tablespoons corn oil

2 tablespoons chopped
   parsley

Method

1. Soak beans in water
   for 8 hours, then boil
   for 40 minutes. Rinse
   with cold water.

2. Crush garlic and mix
   with salt, pepper,
   cumin, lime juice, and
   oil. Add to beans and
   mix. Garnish with
   parsley and serve.

Chickpea Salad

Ingredients
1/4 kilogram chickpeas
2 tablespoons chopped parsley
Salad dressing:
2 tablespoons corn oil
1 tablespoon lime juice
1 teaspoon cumin
1/4 teaspoon salt
1/4 teaspoon pepper
2 cloves garlic, crushed

Method

1. Soak chickpeas in water for 8 hours. Bring to a boil, then simmer for 1 hour. Rinse with cold water.

2. Add salad dressing, garnish with parsley, and serve.

Artichoke Salad

Ingredients
6 artichokes, boiled
Salad dressing (see above for recipe)
1 tablespoon parsley, chopped

Method

1. Quarter artichokes and clean (see page 77).

2. Add salad dressing, garnish with parsley, and serve.

Cabbage Salad

Ingredients
2 or 3 white cabbage leaves
Salt and pepper
1 teaspoon cumin
1 tablespoon mustard
1 tablespoon corn oil
1 tablespoon lime juice

Method

1. Finely slice cabbage leaves. Place in hot water for 10 minutes, drain, then set aside.

2. Prepare dressing by mixing the rest of the ingredients. Toss with cabbage and serve.

Cauliflower Salad

Ingredients
1 small cauliflower
Salt and pepper
1 tablespoon corn oil
1 teaspoon cumin
1 tablespoon lime juice
1 tablespoon chopped parsley

Method

1. Boil cauliflower, cut into medium pieces, and arrange on a plate.

2. Prepare dressing and mix with cauliflower. Garnish with parsley and serve.

Lentil Salad

Ingredients

1/4 kilogram brown
   lentils, boiled
2 cloves garlic
Salt and pepper
1 teaspoon cumin
1 tablespoon lime juice
2 tablespoons corn oil

Method

1. Soak lentils for 4
   hours, then boil for 30
   minutes until cooked.
   Rinse with cold water.

2. Crush garlic, salt, pepper, and cumin. Add
   lime juice and oil. Mix
   dressing with lentils
   and serve.

Tahini Salad

Ingredients
2 cloves garlic
1 teaspoon cumin
Salt and pepper
1/4 cup white tahini   (sesame seed paste)
1 tablespoon lime juice
1 tablespoon vinegar
2 tablespoons water
1 tablespoon chopped   parsley

Method

1. Crush garlic, cumin, salt, and pepper. Add to tahini in a mixing bowl. Add lime juice and vinegar and mix all ingredients well, beating with a spoon in a circular fashion until color turns pale.

2. Add water gradually until the desired consistency is reached.

3. Serve in small dishes and garnish with parsley.

Tahini and Chickpea Salad

Ingredients
1/2 cup boiled chickpeas
1 recipe tahini salad   (above)

Method

1. Puree chickpeas and add to tahini salad.

2. Blend all ingredients and serve in small dishes garnished with parsley, and some whole chickpeas.

Yogurt Salad

Ingredients
2 cloves garlic
1/4 teaspoon salt
1 cup yogurt
1 tablespoon lime juice
1 teaspoon dried mint

Method

1. Crush garlic and salt and mix with yogurt.

2. Season with lime juice and place in small serving dish. Garnish with dried mint and serve.

Tahini Eggplant Salad
(Baba ghanug)

Ingredients

1/2 kilogram eggplants
1 recipe tahini salad
(page 274)
1 tablespoon chopped
parsley

Method

1. Boil whole eggplants. Peel and mash with a fork.

2. Mix crushed eggplant and tahini salad well and place in a serving dish. Garnish with parsley.

Yogurt Cucumber Salad

Ingredients

2 cucumbers
Salt
1 recipe yogurt salad
(opposite)
1 teaspoon dried mint

Method

1. Peel and grate cucumbers. Sprinkle with salt and set aside for 5 minutes to get rid of excess liquid. Drain.

2. Add cucumbers to yogurt salad. Mix well. Garnish with dried mint and serve.

Eggplant Salad with Vinegar and Garlic

Ingredients

1/2 kilogram eggplants
2 sweet or hot chili
    peppers (according
    to taste)
1 cup oil for deep frying
2 cloves garlic
1/4 teaspoon salt
1 tablespoon lime juice
1 tablespoon vinegar
1 tablespoon chopped
    parsley

Method

1. Cut eggplant and peppers into slices. Deep fry in oil (about 5 cm deep), then place in a deep dish.

2. Crush garlic and salt. Add lime juice and vinegar and season eggplant with this mixture. Marinate for a short while. Serve garnished with parsley.

Eggplant Salad with Vinegar and Fried Garlic

Ingredients

1/2 kilogram eggplants
2 sweet peppers
1 cup oil for deep frying
2 cloves garlic
1 tablespoon oil
2 tablespoons vinegar

Method

1. Slice eggplants and peppers and deep fry in hot oil (about 5 cm deep).

2. Slice garlic cloves and fry in oil until yellow in color. Add vinegar.

3. Sprinkle garlic and vinegar over fried eggplant and pepper. Serve.

Eggplant Salad with Tomato, Vinegar, and Garlic

Ingredients

1 recipe Eggplant Salad
    with Vinegar and
    Fried Garlic
    (previous recipe)
1 cup tomato juice
Salt and pepper

Method

Same as previous recipe except after frying garlic, add tomato juice, season with salt and pepper and simmer until sauce thickens. Add vinegar and boil for a few minutes. Pour over eggplant and serve.

Eggplant Yogurt Salad

Ingredients

1/2 kilogram eggplants
1 cup oil for deep frying
2 cloves garlic
1 tablespoon lime juice
Salt and red pepper
1 cup yogurt
2 tablespoons chopped
    parsley

Method

1. Slice eggplants and deep fry in oil (about 5 cm deep). Arrange in a deep dish.

2. Chop garlic, and add lime juice, salt and red pepper, and combine with yogurt. Spoon over eggplant slices and serve garnished with parsley.

Eggplant Stuffed with Garlic and Sweet Pepper

Ingredients

1/2 kilogram small, slender
    black eggplants ('arus)
1/4 kilogram sweet
    peppers, whole
4 cloves garlic
1 hot chili pepper
Salt
1 tablespoon lime juice
1 tablespoon vinegar
2 tablespoons oi

Method

1. Boil eggplants and peppers in salted water for 10 minutes. Rinse with cold water.

2. Crush garlic, hot chili pepper, and salt. Add lime juice.

3. Make a lengthwise cut along the length of each eggplant and stuff with half of the mixture.

4. Arrange eggplants in a serving dish. Season peppers with remaining mixture and arrange with eggplants. Sprinkle with oil and vinegar. Serve.

Salted Herring with Onions and Tomatoes

Ingredients
1 tomato
1 onion
1 hot chili pepper
1 salted herring, skinned and boned
2 tablespoons corn oil
Juice of 2 limes
2 tablespoons tahini (sesame seed paste)
1 tablespoon vinegar
1 tablespoon corn oil

Method

1. Dice tomato, onion, and pepper. Cut herring into bite-sized pieces. Add vegetables.

2. Add oil, lime juice, tahini, and vinegar, stirring to blend ingredients. Sprinkle oil on the top and serve.

Cottage Cheese with Tomatoes
(Gibna falahi bi-l-tamatim)

Ingredients
1/4 kilogram *qarish* cheese
1 tomato
1 hot chili pepper
2 tablespoons corn oil
Juice of 1/2 lime
1/4 teaspoon cumin
1/4 teaspoon red pepper

Method

1. Cube cheese, tomato, and pepper. Combine.

2. Season with oil and lime juice. Sprinkle lightly with cumin and red pepper.

Mature White Cheese
(Gibna qadima or Mish)

Ingredients

1/4 kilogram aged white
   cheese (mish)
2 tablespoons tahini
   (sesame seed paste)
2 tablespoons oil
1 teaspoon lime juice
1 tomato
1 hot chili pepper

Method

1. Cube cheese, tomato,
   tahini, and pepper.
   Combine.

2. Season with oil and
   lime juice. Sprinkle
   lightly with cumin and
   red pepper.

Pickles

Egypt's hot climate necessitates pickles as one means of supplementing the body's salt needs. Vinegar and salt are the main substances used to prepare pickles, and almost all fresh vegetables are available for use all year round. Cucumbers, olives, lemon, pear onions, turnips, and carrots are the most favorite popular pickled vegetables eaten in Egypt.

Pickled Olives

Ingredients

- 1 kilogram large green olives
- 1 head garlic
- 1 bunch celery
- 1/2 kilogram green peppers
- 1/2 kilogram carrots
- 1 tablespoon whole coriander seeds
- 1 kilogram limes (to yield 2 cups lime juice; keep the peels)
- 1 cup coarse-grained salt
- 3 cups water
- 1/4 cup vinegar
- 1/2 cup corn oil

Method

1. Make lengthwise cuts in each olive using a knife or pierce with a fork.

2. Soak olives in water for 2 days, changing the water from time to time. Drain water.

3. Crush unpeeled garlic cloves, chop celery, slice peppers, and grate carrots. Combine these ingredients along with coriander seeds and mix with olives.

4. Place olives in a large glass jar and add 2 cups lime juice, 1 cup salt dissolved in 3 cups water, and the vinegar.

5. Press the olives to the bottom of the jar and cover top with the squeezed lime peels and a layer of oil. Seal well and allow at least 1 month to pickle.

Quick Pickled Limes

Method

Same ingredients and steps of next recipe, but first boil the limes for 5 minutes, then stuff and pickle them. They can then be eaten after two weeks.

Pickled Limes

Ingredients
2 kilograms ripe limes (yellow)
1 tablespoon each safflower sticks, black cumin (habit al-baraka), and salt
1/2 kilogram hot chili peppers
1 cup salt
2 cups water
1 kilogram limes, juiced (keep the peels)
1/2 cup corn oil

Method

1. Wash limes and use a knife to slit each lime on the side.

2. Mix safflower, black cumin, and 1 tablespoon salt. Use mixture to stuff limes.

3. Arrange stuffed limes and chili peppers in alternate layers in a large glass jar.

4. Dissolve 1 cup salt in 2 cups water. Add the lime juice.

5. Cover limes with the salt solution, then with a layer of the lime peels and a layer of oil. Seal jar well and allow at least 1 month to pickle.

Pickled Cucumbers and Peppers

Ingredients

2 cups water
1/4 cup salt
1/4 cup vinegar
4 cloves garlic
1 kilogram small cucumbers
1/2 kilogram hot chili peppers
2 tablespoons oil

Method

1. Boil water and cool. Dissolve salt in water, then add vinegar.

2. Crush unpeeled garlic and add to salt solution.

3. Make a lengthwise slit in each cucumber and place in a glass jar in alternate layers with peppers. Cover with above solution and add a little oil to the top.

4. Seal well and keep for at least 3 days before eating. After opening the jar, store in the refrigerator.

Pickled Turnips (Lift mimallah)

Ingredients

1 kilogram small turnips
1 liter water
1/2 cup coarse-grained salt
1 tablespoon molasses
2 beets

Method

1. Soak turnips in water for 1 hour, then rinse well.

2. Boil water and cool (to avoid froth formation). Add salt and molasses (the molasses prevents the turnips from wilting) to water, and dissolve.

3. Remove the green stems of the turnips, leaving only the base of the green stems. Cut beets into pieces. Place the vegetables in a glass jar, cover with the salted water and seal well. Keep at least 3 days before serving.

Pickled Onions

Ingredients

1 kilogram pearl onions
1 cup water
2 cups vinegar

Method

1. Soak onions in water for 24 hours. Peel and place in a glass jar.

2. Boil 1 cup water, then cool it. Add 2 cups vinegar. Pour over onions, making sure the onions are completely covered. Tightly seal jar.

3. Keep at least 2 weeks before serving.

Pickled Cabbage

Ingredients

1/2 kilogram cabbage
  leaves, boiled
4 cloves garlic
1 tablespoon salt
1/2 teaspoon red pepper
1 liter water, boiled and
  cooled
2 tablespoons vinegar

Method

1. Chop cabbage leaves
   and place in a jar.
   Crush garlic, salt, and
   red pepper and dis-
   solve in cooled water.
   Add vinegar.

2. Cover cabbage with
   above mixture and
   keep 2 days before
   serving.

Pickled Eggplants

Ingredients

1 kilogram slender black
  eggplants *('arus)*
1 head garlic
1 bunch celery, chopped
1 tablespoon salt
1/2 teaspoon red
  pepper
1 cup water, boiled and
  cooled
1/4 cup vinegar
1/2 cup corn oil

Method

1. Boil eggplants, remove
   tops, and slit length-
   wise.

2. Crush together the
   garlic, chopped celery,
   salt, and red pepper
   and use to stuff egg-
   plants.

3. Place stuffed eggplants
   in a jar and add cooled
   water and vinegar.
   Cover top with oil. Seal
   jar tightly and serve
   after 3 days.

Pickled Cauliflower

Ingredients

1/2 kilogram cauliflower
　　florets
1 cup water
1/2 cup vinegar

Method

1. Boil cauliflorets, then rinse with cold water and place in a glass jar.

2. Boil 1 cup water and cool. Add vinegar, then pour over cauliflorets.

3. Seal jar tightly and keep 3 days before serving.

Pickled Carrots

Ingredients

1 kilogram yellow carrots
1/2 cup vinegar
1 cup water, boiled and
　　cooled

Method

1. Wash carrots and cut into long wedges.

2. Add vinegar to cooled water and pour over carrots to completely cover them. Seal jar tightly and keep at least 2 weeks before serving.

Desserts

Egyptian desserts rely on a unique mix of ingredients that yield desserts unlike anything found elsewhere in the Middle-East, such as the mix of molasses, fenugreek seeds, and nuts that create a famous paste (see below), or, if the fenugreek is replaced by black cumin, to make *mifataqa*, both a dessert and a bodily cure. Even flour-based desserts are nutritious and easy to make using the simple ingredients of flour, sugar, and water. Some of the most famous desserts in Egypt are *kunafa* and *qatai'f*, which are closely associated with Ramadan (the Islamic month of fasting). These can be served in many different ways, with nuts, cream, or even with cheese or ground meat to make a savory dish.

Fenugreek Paste *(Hilba ma'quda)*

Method

1. Toast fenugreek seeds and grind them finely. Set aside.

2. Heat 3/4 of the oil and lightly fry sesame seeds until golden in color.

Add flour and stir until flour turns yellow. Add molasses, stirring constantly. Boil for 10 minutes.

3. Add ground fenugreek to the above mixture and stir for 5 minutes. Remove from heat.

4. Toast hazelnuts and remove the skins. Fry in the remaining oil until golden in color and add both to paste. Cool and store in tightly sealed jars.

Ingredients

Ingredients
1/4 kilogram fenugreek seeds
1 liter corn oil
1/4 kilogram sesame seeds
1/4 kilogram flour
2 liters molasses
1/4 kilogram shelled hazelnuts, whole

Note: This recipe makes around 4 large jars of fenugreek paste, to be consumed like jam. This amount can last several months.

Black Cumin Paste

(Mufattaqa)

Ingredients

1/4 kilogram black cumin
seeds *(habit al-baraka)*
1 liter corn oil
1/4 kilogram sesame
seeds
1/4 kilogram flour
2 liters molasses
1/2 kilogram shelled
hazelnuts

Method

1. Clean and pick
the cumin seeds by
removing any stones
or debris. Toast and
grind finely.

2. Follow same steps as
for Fenugreek Paste
(page 289).

al-Malwa'

Ingredients

20 grams sesame seeds
1 cup corn oil
1/8 kilogram flour
1/2 liter molasses
4 teaspoons ground
cinnamon

Mahlab Paste

Ingredients

1/8 kilogram sesame seeds
1/4 kilogram ghee
1/8 kilogram flour
1 liter honey
1/8 kilogram *mahlab*
1/4 kilogram shelled
hazelnuts

Method

1. Fry sesame seeds
lightly in ghee. Add
flour and cook until
color turns yellow.

2. Add honey, stirring
constantly until boiling.

3. Grind *mahlab* and add
to honey, stirring until
consistency thickens.
Remove from heat.

4. Toast hazelnuts and
chop coarsely. Add to
mahlab paste. Store in
a tightly sealed jar.

Method

1. Fry sesame in oil until
golden in color. Add
flour, stirring constantly
until flour turns yellow.

2. Add molasses and
boil for 5 minutes. Add
cinnamon and remove
from heat.

'Asida

Ingredients

1/2 kilogram flour
2 cups water
1/4 kilogram ghee
1/4 liter molasses
1/4 kilogram shelled,
toasted, chopped
hazelnuts

Method

1. Dissolve flour in cold
water. Place over low
heat, stirring continu-
ously until mixture
thickens.

2. Pour in a serving dish.
With the back of a
spoon, create a well in
the middle. Place the
ghee in the well while
the *'asida* is still hot.

3. Drizzle molasses on
the top, then sprinkle
with toasted hazelnuts.
Serve.

3. Cool, then store in
clean jars. To be eaten
like a jam. Serve.

al-Mafruka   Flour Dessert (Sad al-hanak)

Ingredients

1/4 kilogram fenugreek
  seeds
1 liter water
2 cups flour
1 packet active yeast
  (10 grams)
2 tablespoons ghee
1/4 liter molasses

Method

1. Boil fenugreek seeds
   in water for 10 min-
   utes, then set aside
   overnight.

2. Strain out the seeds,
   reserving the liquid.
   Add flour to 1 1/2 cups
   of fenugreek liquid and
   knead the dough.

3. Prepare active yeast
   as directed on pack-
   age. Add to dough,
   and knead again. Set
   aside in a warm place
   to rise.

4. Shape dough into a
   large disc and bake in
   a medium hot oven.

5. While still hot, cut into
   pieces and crumble
   into a bowl. Mix with
   ghee and molasses
   and shape into fingers.
   Serve.

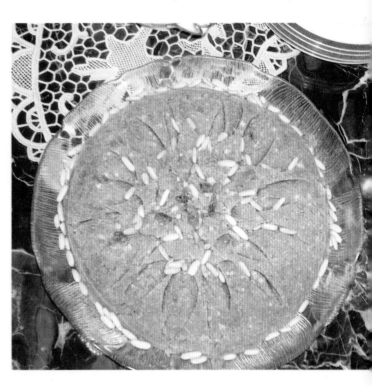

Method

1. Fry flour in ghee until
   lightly browned. Add
   raisins and pine nuts
   and stir into flour.

2. Dissolve sugar in
   water, then add to fried
   flour, stirring until a
   dough forms.

3. Spoon onto a flat serving dish and evenly
   mold into a flower
   shape using a spoon.
   Sprinkle with toasted
   almonds. Serve.

Ingredients

2 cups flour
2 tablespoons ghee
1 tablespoon each raisins
  and pine nuts
1/2 cup sugar
1/2 cup water
2 tablespoons peeled,
  toasted, and chopped
  almonds

Note: Semolina can be used
instead of white flour.

291

Umm 'Ali

Ingredients

1/2 kilogram *ruqaq*
2 tablespoons ghee
1 1/2 liters milk
1 cup sugar
1 cup mixed, whole,
  toasted nuts (hazel-
  nuts, almonds,
  pistachios)
2 tablespoons raisins
2 tablespoons heavy
  cream

Method

1. Break *ruqaq* into
   pieces. Drizzle with
   ghee and bake in a
   medium hot oven until
   golden in color. Place in
   a deep ovenproof dish.

2. Warm the milk.
   Dissolve sugar in it.
   Pour milk over *ruqaq*
   so that it is completely
   covered.

3. Sprinkle toasted nuts
   and raisins on top and
   bake in a medium hot
   oven until liquid is
   absorbed.

4. Remove from oven.
   Add cream and return
   to oven until top is
   lightly browned.
   Serve hot.

Pumpkin Casserole (Qar' Istambuli)

Ingredients

1 kilogram pumpkin

1/4 cup ghee

1 cup raisins

1 cup each coarsely
   crushed pistachios
   and hazelnuts

1 cup sugar

Method

1. Peel pumpkin and cube, removing seeds. Rinse, then fry lightly in ghee. Drain.

2. Spoon pumpkin into a medium pan. Sprinkle with raisins, nuts, and sugar. Cook over low heat, then cover and place in an oven until fully cooked and only a little syrup is left.

3. Spoon into individual plates and serve either warm or cold.

Pumpkin Casserole with Béchamel Sauce

Ingredients

1 kilogram pumpkin
1/2 kilogram sugar
1 cup water

Béchamel sauce:
2 tablespoons flour
2 tablespoons ghee
3 cups milk
1 cup sugar
1 egg
1 teaspoon vanilla powder

Filling:
3 tablespoons chopped
   almonds
1/2 cup raisins
3 tablespoons grated
   coconut
3 tablespoons sugar
2 tablespoons rosewater
1 tablespoon fine dried
   breadcrumbs

Method

1. Peel pumpkin and cube, removing seeds. Add sugar and water. Place over low heat for 30 minutes. Remove from heat and place in a colander to drain excess liquid and sugar.

2. Make béchamel: fry flour in ghee until yellow in color. Add milk and sugar, stirring constantly for about 10 minutes until mixture thickens. Cool.

3. Beat egg and vanilla with a whisk. Add to béchamel and blend.

4. Make filling: combine nuts, raisins, coconut, sugar, and rosewater. Add to cooked pumpkin. Add half the amount of béchamel sauce. Mix these ingredients together.

5. Grease an ovenproof dish. Pour in pumpkin mixture and cover top with remaining béchamel sauce. Sprinkle with the breadcrumbs.

6. Bake in a medium hot oven for 30 minutes until top is lightly browned. Serve.

'Aysh al-saraya

Method

1. Remove the crusts of the bread and cut into 2 cm thick slices.

2. Moisten bread slices with water and arrange in a large round pan (28 cm).

3. Prepare sugar syrup by combining sugar, lime juice, and water and bringing to a boil for about 20 minutes, then cool. (Syrup must be light.)

4. Heat 3 tablespoons sugar and water until mixture is a brown caramel color. Add cold syrup and stir.

5. Place pan containing bread over low heat, gradually adding syrup until it is well absorbed and 'Aysh al-saraya is browned.

6. Wet serving plate. Turn tray over, onto serving dish. Even surface and cool.

7. To serve, cut into triangular pieces and garnish with heavy cream and chopped pistachios.

Ingredients

1 large loaf of English bread (preferably stale)
3 tablespoons sugar
3 tablespoons water
1/2 liter fresh heavy cream
1/4 kilogram chopped pistachios

Sugar syrup:
1 kilogram sugar
Juice of 1 lime
2 cups water

Sweet Potato Casserole with Béchamel Sauce

Ingredients

1 kilogram large sweet potatoes
Same ingredients used for filling and béchamel as in previous recipe (page 295)

Method

1. Boil sweet potatoes, peel, and mash with a fork.

2. Follow steps 2 to 6 of recipe opposite.

Individual 'aysh al-saraya with Heavy Cream

Method

Follow the same steps described opposite, but use a piece of cloth to absorb excess syrup. Using a small cup as a cutter, cut 'aysh al-saraya into small circles. For each serving, use two 'aysh al-saraya circles and spoon heavy cream in between.

Rolled 'aysh al-saraya

Method

Cut 'aysh al-saraya into 3 cm wide strips. Place a piece of cream on one end and roll like a cigar. Garnish outsides with ground pistachios.

Luqmat al-qadi (Zalabia, or Lokomadis in Greek)

Ingredients
1 packet active yeast (10 grams)
1 teaspoon sugar
1 cup warm water
2 cups flour
Oil for deep frying
Powdered sugar
1 tablespoon ground cinnamon
Syrup:
1/2 cup water
1 cup sugar
Juice of 1/2 lime

Method

1. To prepare syrup, combine water, sugar, and lime juice. Cook over heat, stirring until sugar dissolves and syrup reaches the desired, thick consistency. Cool.

2. Prepare yeast by adding sugar to it and dissolving combination in warm water. Set aside in a warm place to prove.

3. Sift flour and mix with yeast and a little water to form a soft dough. Let dough rise for 1 hour.

4. Using a spoon, divide dough into pieces and deep fry in hot oil (about 5 cm deep) until golden brown.

5. After dough pieces are fried, soak them immediately in cold syrup for 1 minute. Remove them with a slotted spoon and place in a colander to drain excess syrup. Sprinkle tops with powdered sugar and cinnamon. Serve.

Balah al-sham

Ingredients

1 cup water
8 tablespoons oil
1 1/2 cups flour
6 eggs
1/4 teaspoon vanilla
  powder
Oil for deep frying
1 large cup sugar syrup,
  cooled (page 296)
2 tablespoons grated
  coconut
Chopped hazelnuts

Method

1. Boil water and oil for a few minutes. Add flour, stirring constantly, until dough forms a single ball around the spoon.

2. Remove dough from heat and rest. Add eggs, one at a time, beating to combine well. Add vanilla.

3. Squeeze dough through a star-tipped pastry bag to form fingers, piping the batter directly into the hot oil. Deep fry in hot oil (about 5 cm deep) until golden brown. Remove with a slotted spoon and place in cold sugar syrup for 1 minute.

4. Drain excess syrup and arrange in a serving plate. Sprinkle with coconut and hazelnuts.

Assabi' Zaynab

Ingredients

1 packet active yeast
  10 grams)
1 teaspoon sugar
1 cup warm water
1 cup ghee
3 cups flour
1 cup semolina flour
Oil for deep frying
1 large cup sugar syrup,
  cooled (page 296)
1/4 teaspoon vanilla
  powder

Method

1. Prepare yeast and proof as previously described in recipe for *luqmat al-qadi* (page 297). Heat ghee, add to flour and semolina flour. Add dissolved yeast and knead well. Allow dough to rise for 1 hour.

2. Shape dough into small balls, a half-egg size each, and flatten. Roll over a fine-toothed grater to give the top its distinctive appearance and roll into short cigar shapes.

3. Deep fry in oil, then place in cooled syrup with vanilla for 1 minute. Drain excess syrup and serve.

Mishabik

Ingredients

1 packet active yeast
(10 grams)
1 teaspoon sugar
1 cup flour
1 cup water
1 cup warm, thick sugar
syrup (page 296)
1 tablespoon rosewater

Method

1. Prepare yeast and proof as in recipe for *luqmat al-qadi* (page 297). Mix flour and water. Add yeast and knead well. Set aside in a warm place to rise.

2. Place batter in a funnel-shaped container. Pour an outline circle of the batter directly into the oil, continuing to squeeze it in random shapes to fill the circle's center. Turn over onto other side until pale yellow on both sides.

3. Remove from heat and place in the hot syrup to which the rosewater was added.

4. After cooling them, wrap *mishabik* discs in cellophane paper to preserve softness.

Kunafa with Nuts

Ingredients

1/2 kilogram *kunafa*
1/2 cup ghee
1 cup hazelnuts or
walnuts
2 cups sugar syrup,
cooled (page 296)

Method

1. Cut *kunafa* into small pieces. Rub with half the amount of ghee until absorbed.

2. Grease a round pan with ghee and add half the *kunafa*. Press firmly by using the bottom of a smaller pan.

3. Toast nuts, then chop them. Sprinkle over *kunafa* in pan, then cover with remaining *kunafa*. Press firmly and drizzle remaining ghee on top.

4. Bake in a medium hot oven for 30 minutes or until top is golden brown.

5. Remove from oven and drizzle cooled syrup evenly over the whole pan. Return to hot oven for another 5 minutes, after turning off the heat.

6. Garnish *kunafa* with chopped nuts. Cut into triangles and serve.

Fried *Kunafa* with Heavy Cream

Ingredients
1/2 kilogram *kunafa*
1/2 cup ghee
1 cup hot water
2 cups sugar syrup, cooled (page 296)
2 tablespoons toasted and chopped pistachios
1/2 liter fresh heavy cream

Method

1. Cut *kunafa* into small pieces and fry in ghee, stirring until golden brown in color.

2. Place in colander to drain, then pour hot water over *kunafa* to get rid of excess ghee.

3. Pour sugar syrup over *kunafa* and drain excess.

4. Sprinkle pistachios in the bottom of a round tray. Arrange half the *kunafa* over it.

5. Spoon heavy cream onto the *kunafa*, then add remaining *kunafa* and press lightly. Turn over onto a glass plate. Serve.

Kunafa with Pudding

Ingredients
1/2 kilogram *kunafa*
1/2 cup ghee
2 cups sugar syrup, cooled (page 296)
Pudding filling:
1 packet vanilla pudding
1/2 cup sugar
2 cups milk
1 tablespoon grated coconut

Method

1. Prepare pudding. Dissolve powder and sugar in cold milk, then cook over medium heat, stirring until mixture thickens. Cool slightly, then add coconut and stir.

2. Cut *kunafa* into small pieces. Add half the ghee and rub well until absorbed.

3. Grease a round pan (30 cm) with a little ghee. Place half the *kunafa* in the bottom and press firmly. Spread the pudding evenly, then add remaining *kunafa*. Drizzle remaining ghee on the top.

4. Bake in a medium hot oven for 30 minutes, until top is lightly browned.

5. Pour cold syrup onto *kunafa* and return to hot, turned off oven for another 5 minutes. Serve.

Kunafa with Ricotta Cheese

Ingredients

1/2 kilogram *kunafa*
1/2 cup ghee
2 cups sugar syrup,
    cooled (page 296)

Filling:
1/4 kilogram ricotta
    cheese
1 tablespoon ghee

Method

Same as previous recipe, but replace pudding with ricotta.

Qata'if with Pudding

Filling:
1 cup prepared pudding
2 tablespoons grated
    coconut
1/2 kilogram *qata'if*
1 large cup sugar syrup,
    cooled (page 296)

Method

Same as above recipe.

Qata'if with Nuts

Ingredients

1/2 kilogram *qata'if*
2 tablespoons ghee
1/4 cup corn oil
1 large cup sugar syrup,
    cooled (page 296)

Filling:
1 cup mixture of hazelnuts
    and walnuts, chopped
2 tablespoons sugar
2 tablespoons raisins

Method

1. Combine filling ingredients and use to fill individual *qata'if* (*qata'if* are similar to small pancakes). Fold over and seal edges, pressing firmly.

2. Deep fry individual *qata'if* pieces in ghee and oil combined, then place in cold syrup for 1 minute. Remove and drain excess syrup. Place in a deep dish and serve.

Qata'if with Heavy Cream and Nuts

Ingredients

1/2 kilogram *qata'if*
2 tablespoons ghee
2 tablespoons corn oil
1 cup sugar syrup, cooled
    (page 296)
1/2 liter fresh heavy
    cream
2 tablespoons chopped
    pistachios

Method

1. Shape individual *qata'if* pieces into cones. Wet edges with water and seal well.

2. Fry in ghee and oil combined until golden yellow in color. Remove and place in cool syrup.

3. Fill cones with heavy cream and sprinkle with pistachios. Arrange on a plate and serve.

Note: *kunafa* and *qata'if* can be found in special shops called 'kunafa shops' or in supermarkets.

Baklava
with Nuts

Ingredients

1 cup ghee

1/2 kilogram gulash
(filo dough)

1 cup chopped hazelnuts
or walnuts

1 tablespoon sugar

1 large cup sugar syrup,
cooled (page 296)

Method

1. Coat a rectangular
   pan (34 x 22 cm)
   with ghee. Arrange
   gulash sheets in
   layers,coating sheets
   lightly with ghee.

2. Mix nuts and sugar
   and sprinkle over lay-
   ered gulash. Arrange
   remaining gulash as
   in previous step.

3. Using a sharp knife,
   cut gulash diagonally
   into small diamond
   shapes. Drizzle with
   hot ghee.

4. Bake in a medium
   hot oven until top is
   golden in color. Pour
   cold syrup over it and
   return to turned off hot
   oven for 5 minutes.
   Serve.

Baklava with Pudding

(Namura)

Ingredients

1 cup ghee

1/2 kilogram gulash (filo dough)

2 cups sugar syrup, cooled (page 296)

Filling:

2 tablespoons cornstarch

1 cup milk

1 tablespoon ghee

1 teaspoon rosewater

1 tablespoon grated coconut

Method

1. Make filling: dissolve cornstarch in cold milk. Place over heat, stirring constantly until mixture thickens. Add 1 tablespoon ghee, rosewater, and coconut. Cool.

2. Follow the same steps as on page 304. Spread the pudding over the layered gulash exactly in the middle, then arrange the rest of the gulash sheets, but cut into larger diamonds.

Higaziyya

Method

1. Combine flour and semolina. Add ghee and oil and rub with fingertips until fats are completely absorbed.

2. Prepare yeast by adding sugar to it and dissolving combination in warm water. Add to above ingredients.

3. Prepare filling by combining ingredients.

4. Coat a rectangular pan (34 x 22 cm) with ghee. Place half the dough in the bottom and spread evenly. Sprinkle on the filling, then cover with remaining dough. Even out dough using hands. Use a fork to make horizontal and vertical stripes along top to give the *higaziyya* its characteristic appearance.

5. Bake in a medium hot oven until top is lightly browned and *higaziyya* is done. Cool, then cut into squares and serve.

Ingredients

3 cups flour

1 cup fine semolina

1 cup ghee

1/2 cup corn oil

1 packet active yeast (10 grams)

1 teaspoon sugar

1 cup warm water

Filling:

1 cup chopped hazelnuts

5 tablespoons sugar

1 tablespoon cinnamon

1 teaspoon rosewater

Cornmeal (Maize) Cake with Pitted Dates

Method

1. Beat ghee and oil well with a hand held whisk or electric mixer until light and fluffy. Add sugar gradually, then eggs and vanilla, beating continuously the whole time.

2. Sift cornmeal, flour, and baking powder. Add to above mixture and stir.

3. Add milk or orange juice, until a thick batter forms.

4. Grease a rectangular pan (34 x 22 cm) with ghee and sprinkle with flour. Pour half the batter into the pan.

5. Using palms of hand, flatten pitted dates into thin patties and lay out over batter. Cover with remaining batter. Even out batter with the smooth edge of a knife.

Ingredients
3/4 cup ghee
1/2 cup corn oil
1 1/2 cups sugar
3 eggs
1 packet vanilla powder (10 grams)
3 cups cornmeal
1 cup white flour
1 packet baking powder
1/2 cup milk or orange juice
1/2 kilogram pitted dates

6. Bake in a medium hot oven for 45 minutes, lowering the heat when the batter rises. Remove when top is lightly browned.

7. Cut into rectangular pieces about 3 cm wide and serve warm.

Coconut Dessert *(Basima)*

Ingredients
1/4 kilogram ghee
1/2 kilogram sugar
1/2 liter milk
1 cup flour
1/2 kilogram coconut
1 tablespoon baking powder

Method

1. Melt ghee over medium heat. Add sugar and milk, stirring well until sugar dissolves. Set aside to cool.

2. Combine flour, coconut, and baking powder and add to above mixture. Mix ingredients.

3. Grease an oven pan (34 x 22 cm) with a thick coat of ghee. Pour batter into pan, even out with hands and cut diagonally into diamond shapes.

4. Bake in a medium hot oven for 15 minutes, then cool. Serve.

Cake with Yogurt

Ingredients

3 eggs
1/2 teaspoon vanilla
    powder
1 cup yogurt
1 cup sugar
1 cup flour
Ghee
1 packet baking powder
1 cup sugar syrup, cooled
    (page 296)
1/4 liter heavy cream

Method

1. Beat eggs and vanilla. Add yogurt and sugar, beating continuously with a wire whisk or electric beater.

2. Sift flour and baking powder. Add to above mixture and stir.

3. Coat a pan (30 cm) with ghee and flour. Pour batter into pan and bake in a medium hot oven for 45 minutes until top is lightly browned.

4. Remove from oven and immediately pour cold syrup onto cake. Allow a few minutes for syrup to be absorbed, then . cut into squares. Serve with heavy cream.

Sponge Cake

Method

1. Beat ghee and sugar on high speed with an electric mixer, adding eggs and vanilla and beating until mixture becomes somewhat thick. Sift flour and baking powder. Add to above mixture and stir. Gradually add milk or juice.

2. Grease a pan (30 cm) with ghee and sprinkle lightly with flour. Pour batter into tray.

3. Bake in a medium hot oven for 15 minutes. Lower heat and bake for another 30 minutes until top is lightly browned.

Ingredients

3/4 cup ghee
1 1/2 cups sugar
5 eggs
1/4 teaspoon vanilla
    powder
3 cups flour
1 tablespoon baking
    powder
1 cup milk or orange juice

4. Turn over onto a wire sifter or rack. Cool in a draft-free place.

Note: You may add chopped, dried fruits (prunes, raisins, apricots) to batter before baking.

309

Shakalama
(Another Coconut Dessert)

Ingredients

2 egg whites
1/2 teaspoon vanilla
   powder
1 1/2 cups powdered sugar
1 1/2 cups flour
1/2 packet baking powder
3 cups finely grated
   coconut
Ghee
1 cup sugar syrup, cooled

Method

1. Beat egg whites and
   vanilla until creamy.
   Add sugar, continuing
   to beat until consistency
   thickens.

2. Combine flour, baking
   powder, and coconut.
   Add to above mixture.

3. Grease an oven pan
   (34 x 22 cm) with
   ghee. Spoon mixture
   onto pan and flatten
   out with hands.

4. Bake in a medium hot
   oven until top is lightly
   browned and *shakalama*
   is set. Pour cold syrup
   over hot *shakalama*,
   then cool. Cut and
   serve.

Shakalama Pieces
(Macaruns)

Ingredients

1 cup sweetened
   condensed milk
1/4 kilogram grated
   coconut
1/2 teaspoon vanilla
   powder
1 tablespoon ghee
1 tablespoon flour
1 tablespoon powdered
   sugar

Method

1. Mix condensed milk,
   coconut, and vanilla.

2. Grease a large pan
   with ghee and sprinkle
   with flour and pow-
   dered sugar.

3. Drop dough by spoon-
   fuls in small pyramid
   shapes.

4. Bake in a medium hot
   oven for 5 minutes
   until tops are lightly
   browned. Serve.

Ruwani

Ingredients

10 eggs
1/2 teaspoon vanilla
   powder
1/4 cup sugar
2 cups semolina
Pinch of salt
3/4 cup ghee
1 cup light sugar syrup,
   cooled (page 296)
1/4 liter heavy cream

Method

1. Beat eggs and vanilla.
   Add sugar gradually
   and continue beating.

2. Combine semolina
   flour and salt. Melt
   ghee and add to the
   flour and salt. Mix with
   fingers until a thick batter forms.

3. Coat a tray (30 cm)
   with ghee and flour.
   Pour above mixture
   into tray.

4. Bake in a medium hot
   oven until top is lightly
   browned. Drizzle with
   cold syrup while still
   hot.

5. Cut into squares and
   garnish with heavy
   cream. Serve.

Harisa

Ingredients

1 kilogram semolina flour
1/2 kilogram sugar
1 cup ghee
1 cup water
2 tablespoons tahini
   (sesame seed paste)
1 large cup sugar syrup
   (page 296)
1/2 teaspoon vanilla
   powder
Whole, toasted hazelnuts,
   optional

Method

1. Mix semolina flour, sugar, 1/2 cup ghee, and water to form a dough.

2. Generously grease a rectangular pan (34 x 22 cm) with ghee. Spread tahini on the bottom of the pan, then spread dough on top.

3. Bake in a medium hot oven for 30 minutes until top is lightly browned.

4. Heat syrup and add the remaining 1/2 cup ghee and vanilla. Pour over *harisa* after removing from oven, then return to hot oven for another 5 minutes.

5. Cool slightly, then cut and serve.

Note: You may decorate the top before baking with whole toasted hazelnuts.

311

Rashidiyya

Ingredients

1 1/2 cups fine cornstarch
2 cups water
1 cup powdered sugar
2 tablespoons rosewater
1/2 cup pomegranate juice
1/2 cup ghee
1/2 cup raisins
1/2 cup pistachios

Method

1. Dissolve cornstarch in water along with sugar, rosewater, and pomegranate juice.

2. Heat ghee to boiling. Add above mixture, stirring over medium heat until a dough forms.

3. Lower heat and continue stirring from time to time until dough starts to crumble.

4. Add raisins and pistachios and serve hot.

Note: Pomegranate juice is added to give the dough its distinct purple color.

Basbusa with Yogurt

Ingredients
2 cups fine semolina flour
1 1/2 cups sugar
2 tablespoons ghee
2 teaspoons baking powder
1 cup yogurt
2 tablespoons tahini (sesame seed paste)
1/4 cup peeled almonds
2 cups sugar syrup (page 296) to which 2 tablespoons ghee are added

Method

1. Rub together semolina, sugar, 1 tablespoon ghee, and baking powder. Mix with yogurt.

2. Coat a rectangular pan with 1 tablespoon ghee and tahini. Pour above mix into pan (34 x 22 cm) and even out with hands. Cut into squares and place an almond in the center of each square.

3. Bake in a medium hot oven for 45 minutes until tops are lightly browned. Pour warm syrup over hot *basbusa* and return to hot oven for 5 minutes.

4. Cool and serve.

Pudding with Pistachios *(Mihalabiya)*

Ingredients
3/4 cup sugar
3 tablespoons cornstarch
1 tablespoon rosewater
3 cups milk
Some chopped pistachios

Method

1. Dissolve sugar, cornstarch, and rosewater in cold milk. Place over low heat, stirring constantly until mixture thickens.

2. Pour into small serving dishes or cups. Cool, garnish with pistachios, and serve.

Rice Pudding *(Urz bi-l-laban)*

Ingredients

1/2 cup rice
1 cup water
1 1/2 cups sugar
2 tablespoons cornstarch
3 cups milk
1 tablespoon rosewater
1 cup chopped nuts
2 teaspoons cinnamon

Method

1. Boil rice in water. Dissolve sugar and starch in cold milk and add rosewater. Pour mixture onto rice, stirring constantly until boiling.

2. Lower heat and simmer for 15 minutes, stirring occasionally.

3. Pour into serving dishes and cool.

4. Garnish top with nuts and cinnamon. Serve.

Ground Rice Pudding

Ingredients

1/2 cup ground rice
2 tablespoons cornstarch
1 1/2 cups sugar
3 cups milk
2 teaspoons rosewater
1 tablespoon cinnamon
2 tablespoons ground
  pistachios

Method

1. Combine rice, corn-starch, sugar, milk, and rosewater, beating well with a wire whisk. Place over heat, stir-ring constantly until it comes to a boil.

2. Simmer over low heat for 15 minutes, stirring from time to time. Pour into small serving dishes and cool. Garnish with cinnamon and pista-chios and serve.

Poor Man's Kishk *(Kishk al-fuqara')*

Method

1. Soak almonds in cold water for 1 hour, then remove outer peel. Soak coconut in 1/4 cup milk for 1 hour, then strain and squeeze out excess milk.

2. Grind almonds and mix with coconut. Dissolve in 6 cups milk along with sugar. Place over medium heat and bring to a boil.

3. Dissolve starch in 1/4 cup milk. Add to above mixture, stirring over low heat for 5 minutes until consistency thickens.

Ingredients

1/4 kilogram almonds
1 cup grated coconut
6 1/2 cups milk
1 cup sugar
1 cup rice starch
1 tablespoon rosewater
1/4 cup chopped
  pistachios

4. Add rosewater and remove from heat. Pour into a deep dish and cool. Garnish top with chopped pistachios and coconut. Serve.

Whole Wheat Pudding
(‘Ashura)

Ingredients

1/2 kilogram whole wheat
   grains
1 1/2 liters milk
3 cups sugar
1/2 cup fine cornstarch
1 tablespoon rosewater
1/2 cup raisins
1/2 cup boiled, peeled,
   toasted almond halves
2 tablespoons grated
   coconut

Method

1. Starting the night before, soak wheat in water for 8 hours then boil for 2 hours. Leave grains in hot water overnight.

2. The following day, puree half the amount of cooked grains with the cooking water. Leave the remaining half whole.

3. Combine the milk, sugar, cornstarch, and rosewater with both pureed and whole grains and cook over medium heat until consistency thickens. Add raisins.

4. Pour into small, deep dishes and garnish with toasted almonds and coconut. Cool and serve.

Apricot Pudding *(Mihalabiyat qamar al-din)*

Ingredients

1/2 kilogram pressed
   apricot sheets
   (qamar al-din)
1 cup sugar
1/2 cup fine cornstarch
1/2 cup water
1/2 cup raisins
1/2 cup dried apricot
   halves, chopped
2 tablespoons grated
   coconut
2 tablespoons ground nuts

Method

1. Cut apricot sheets into small pieces and place in saucepan. Add sugar and cover with water. Boil for 10 minutes, then set aside for 30 minutes. Sieve mixture.

2. Dissolve cornstarch in water, then add to sieved apricot. Boil, stirring constantly until mixture thickens. Add raisins and dried apricot halves. Boil for a few minutes.

3. Spoon into small serving dishes. Garnish with coconut and ground nuts. Cool and serve.

Note: You may prepare the above recipe using 2 cups of orange juice and 1/2 kilogram carrots (boiled and pureed) instead of the pressed apricot sheets.

Apple Compote *(Khushaf al-tuffah)*

Ingredients
1 kilogram apples
Juice of 1 lime
1 cup sugar
1 liter water

Method

1. Peel and core apples. Cut into slices. Soak in water to which the juice of 1 lime has been added.

2. Dissolve sugar in 1 liter water and bring to a boil. Add apples and simmer over low heat until fully cooked. Remove any froth that forms.

3. Cool. Spoon into porcelain plates and serve.

Note: Many different fruit compotes can be prepared this way using pears, apricots, and peaches.

319

Dried Fruit Compote
(Khushaf fakha mugafafa)

Ingredients
1 cup sugar
1 liter water
1 teaspoon lime juice
1/2 cup prunes
1/2 cup dried apricots
6 dried figs
1/2 cup dried dates
1/2 cup large raisins
2 tablespoons pine nuts
1/2 cup Almonds, boiled for 10 minutes, peeled and halved

Method

1. Combine sugar, water, and lime juice. Boil to a light syrup, removing any froth that forms.

2. Wash dried fruits, divide figs in half and add all to boiling syrup. Boil for 5 minutes.

3. Set aside for at least 1 hour in the hot syrup. Add pine nuts and almonds. Refrigerate.

Prunes with Cream

Ingredients

1/4 kilogram sugar
1 liter water
Juice of 1/2 lime
1/2 kilogram prunes
2 tablespoons pine nuts
1/8 kilogram boiled,
    peeled almonds
1/2 liter light cream

Method

1. Combine sugar, water, and lime juice. Bring to a boil, stirring, then simmer to a light syrup. Remove any froth that forms.

2. Wash prunes and add to syrup. Boil for 10 minutes over low heat until syrup thickens. Cool.

3. Add pine nuts and almonds to prunes. Cool.

4. Before serving, spoon into small dishes and garnish with fresh cream.

Brioche

Ingredients

2 packets active yeast
   (20 grams)

1 kilogram flour

Pinch of salt

1/4 teaspoon mastic
   grains

1/4 teaspoon *mahalib*

1 1/2 cups sugar

5 eggs

1 cup butter, at room
   temperature

1 1/2 cups milk

1/4 cup raisins

1 egg, beaten with vanilla

Extra sugar

Method

1. Prepare active yeast as directed on packet. Sift flour and add salt.

2. Finely grind mastic grains and *mahalib*. Combine with flour and sugar.

3. Beat eggs and add to mixture. Add butter. Mix all ingredients well, and add milk.

4. Add yeast and knead well. Mix the rasins in. Set aside in a warm place for around an hour to rise.

5. Divide dough into equal egg-sized pieces. Shape into 1 1/2 cm-thick ropes and twist each one into a circle to look like a snail's shell.

6. Brush top with beaten egg and sprinkle with sugar. Set aside to rise for about another hour. Bake in a medium hot oven until top is lightly browned for 30 minutes.

Cookies with Pitted Dates *(Quras bi-l-'agwa)*

Ingredients

1 kilogram flour

1/4 teaspoon salt

1/8 kilogram sesame
    seeds

1 cup corn oil

1 cup ghee

1/8 kilogram anise seeds

2 packets active yeast
    (20 grams)

1 cup warm water for
    kneading

Filling:

1/2 kilogram pitted dates

1 tablespoon ghee

1 tablespoon sesame
    seeds

Method

1. Sift flour and salt and place in a deep metal bowl. Make a well in the flour and add 1/8 kilogram cleaned sesame seeds.

2. Heat oil and 1 cup ghee to boiling and pour gradually over sesame seeds, stirring until they turn golden in color.

3. Mix ingredients with a spoon until flour absorbs ghee. Add anise seeds and mix well.

4. Prepare yeast as directed on packet. Add to flour and knead, adding warm water as required. Allow dough to rise for about 1 hour. Divide into small balls, about 36.

5. Make filling: mince dates and mix with 1 tablespoon ghee and 1 tablespoon sesame seeds. Shape into about 36 small balls.

6. Fill dough balls with date balls, then flatten dough into discs using the palms of the hands.

7. Bake in a hot oven for 15 minutes until tops are lightly browned.

Cookies with Nuts
(Ma'mul)

Ingredients
2 packets active yeast (20 grams)
1 cup semolina flour
2 cups flour
1/4 teaspoon salt
3/4 cup ghee
1 cup warm water, for kneading
Filling:
1/2 cup semolina flour
1/2 cup sugar
1 cup crushed hazelnuts
1 tablespoon cinnamon
2 tablespoons rosewater

Method

1. Prepare yeast as directed on packet. Sift two flours together with salt. Add ghee and mix with fingertips until absorbed. Add yeast and knead well, adding warm water as needed until a moldable dough forms.

2. Rise in a warm place for 1 hour, then divide into 25 pieces of equal size, each about the size of an egg.

3. Combine ingredients for filling. Stuff filling into individual dough pieces and shape into patties. Use a fork to make crisscross markings on the top of each.

4. Bake in a hot oven for 30 minutes until top is lightly browned. Serve.

Ma'mul Biscuits with Pitted Dates
(Ma'mul bi-l-'agwa)

Filling:
1/2 kilogram pitted dates
1 tablespoon ghee

Method

Same as previous recipe.

325

Ka'k with Pitted Dates

Ingredients

6 cups flour

1/4 teaspoon salt

10 grams *ka'k* spice
(consists of *mahalib*,
cinnamon, cloves,
cardamon, camphor,
and java pepper),
optional

1/8 kilogram sesame
seeds

2 large cups ghee

2 packets active yeast
(20 grams) and 1
teaspoon sugar

Warm water for kneading

1 kilogram powdered
sugar

Filling:

1 kilogram pitted dates

1 tablespoon ghee

1 tablespoon sesame
seeds

Method

1. Sift flour, salt, and *ka'k* spice. Place in a metal bowl. Clean sesame seeds by removing any stones or sand in the seeds, and place in a well in the middle of the flour.

2. Heat ghee to boiling and add gradually to sesame seeds, stirring until color is golden. Stir ghee into flour with a spoon until well absorbed.

3. Prepare yeast with sugar and warm water as directed on packet, and knead into dough, adding warm water as necessary, so that dough can be shaped easily.

4. Make filling: grind dates finely using a grinder, and mix with 1 tablespoon ghee and 1 tablespoon sesame seeds. Shape into short ropes.

5. Divide dough into equal pieces and shape into ropes. Flatten the ropes until they are 5 cm wide. Place the date ropes in the middle of the pieces of dough then seal the rope edges. Use the rope of dough to make a circle. Use serrated cookie tweezers or the back of a fork to make decorative markings along the sealed edges. Set aside to rise.

6. Bake in a medium hot oven for 15 minutes, then cool.

7. Sprinkle with powdered sugar and serve.

Note: *Ka'k* are a type of biscuit typically prepared for feasts.

Ka'k with 'Agamiyya

Method

1. Fry sesame seeds in ghee until golden brown. Add flour and stir until color becomes yellow.

2. Add honey, stirring well, then add water and stir until a dough is formed. Cool.

3. Roughly chop walnuts and mix into prepared 'agamiya. Use small pieces to stuff small balls of ka'k dough. Flatten ka'k balls with palms of the hand and set aside to rise.

4. Bake and sprinkle with powdered sugar as described in previous recipe.

Ingredients
Same as recipe on page 327 but replace the date filling with the following ingredients for 'Agamiyya filling.

'Agamiyya filling:
3 tablespoons sesame seeds
3 tablespoons ghee
3 tablespoons flour
3 cups honey
3 tablespoons warm water
1/4 kilogram shelled walnuts

Cookies with Anise Seeds

Ingredients
4 eggs
1 packet vanilla powder (10 grams)
1 cup powdered sugar
2 1/2 cups flour
1 packet baking powder
2 tablespoons anise seeds
1/3 cup corn oil

Method

1. Beat eggs and vanilla well. Gradually add sugar, beating until mixture is fluffy.

2. Sift flour and baking powder together, then add anise seeds. Combine all ingredients and knead to form a relatively soft dough.

3. Grease a rectangular pan (39 x 29 cm) with oil and pour the above mixture into it. Bake in a medium hot oven for 30 minutes, then cool.

4. Cut into bars and arrange in several large pans with spaces between each bar. Return to oven for another 15 minutes until bars are lightly browned and crisp.

Ghurayiba (Cookies)

Ingredients

1/2 kilogram ghee
1/4 cup powdered sugar
6 cups flour
1 large cup peeled
  almonds or whole
  cloves

Method

1. Beat ghee with electric mixer for 15 minutes, adding sugar gradually until ghee is light and fluffy.

2. Sift flour and add gradually, stirring until flour is fully absorbed.

3. Shape dough into small balls, pressing an almond or a clove in the center of each ball.

4. Bake in a warm oven for 10 minutes.

Note: The baking should not change the color of the dough.

Petit Four Cookies

Ingredients

3/4 kilogram butter
1/4 kilogram powdered
  sugar
8 eggs
1 packet vanilla powder
  (10 grams)
1 kilogram flour
1 packet baking powder
2 tablespoons
  unsweetened cocoa
1 jar Apricot jam (about
  250 grams)
Ground nuts, grated
  coconut, and grated
  chocolate

Method

1. Beat butter with electric mixer until light and fluffy, adding sugar gradually.

2. Beat eggs and vanilla well. Add to the above mixture and stir.

3. Sift flour and baking powder. Add gradually to the above mixture to form a dough that can be molded.

4. Divide the dough in half. Place one half in a pastry bag with a large serrated tip and pipe out into flower shapes on a baking sheet.

5. Mix the other half with cocoa and repeat process.

6. Bake petit fours in a medium hot oven for 15 minutes, then cool.

7. Using a teaspoon and apricot jam, stick each two petit fours together (one white and one brown). Decorate edges with ground nuts, grated coconut, or grated chocolate.

Cururia Cookies

Ingredients

1 kilogram flour
1 cup sugar
Pinch of salt
1 cup ghee
1/2 cup corn oil
2 packets active yeast (20 grams)
1 teaspoon sugar
1 cup warm water
1 cup warm water for kneading
1 egg
1 teaspoon vanilla powder

Method

1. Sift flour, sugar, and salt together and place in a deep metal bowl. Heat ghee and oil to boiling and pour over flour. Mix with a spoon until absorbed, then set aside to cool.

2. Prepare yeast as directed on packet with 1 teaspoon sugar and 1 cup warm water. Add to mixture. Knead with 1 cup warm water, adding more water if needed. Set aside to rise, then divide into small pieces. Shape pieces into short ropes, then twist to form S shapes.

3. Beat egg and vanilla together, and brush on top. Rise for 1 hour.

4. Bake in a medium hot oven for 15 minutes until tops are lightly browned. Serve.

Ammonia Cookies

Method

1. Beat ghee, oil, and sugar with electric mixer. Add eggs and vanilla, beating continuously until mixture is light and creamy.

2. Warm the milk. Using a deep bowl, dissolve ammonia in milk. Add to above mixture.

3. Sift flour and baking powder and mix with above ingredients to form a dough.

4. Shape individual biscuits using a cookie press and arrange on a baking tray.

5. Brush top with egg beaten with vanilla and bake in a medium hot oven for 10 minutes until tops are lightly browned.

Ingredients

1 large cup ghee or butter
1/4 cup corn oil
1/3 kilogram powdered sugar
10 eggs
1 teaspoon vanilla powder
1 cup milk
1 tablespoon ammonia (raising agent)
1 kilogram flour
1 tablespoon baking powder
1 egg beaten with 1 teaspoon vanilla powder

Lancashire Cookies

Ingredients

1 cup ghee
1 cup sugar
3 eggs
1 packet vanilla powder
  (10 grams)
3 cups flour
1 packet baking powder
1 cup corn meal
2 tablespoons unsweet-
  ened cocoa
Apricot jam
Grated chocolate

Method

1. Beat ghee well using an electric mixer. Add sugar gradually, then eggs and vanilla, beating continuously.

2. Combine flour, baking powder, and cornflour and mix into above mixture until a dough that can be molded is formed.

3. Divide dough in half and add cocoa to one part.

4. Shape dough into small balls and arrange on a tray (39x29 cm).

5. Bake in a low oven for 10 minutes, then cool.

6. Using apricot jam, stick each two biscuits together and decorate sides with grated chocolate.

Qaraqish

Ingredients

3 cups flour
2 tablespoons sesame
  seeds
2 tablespoons ghee
1/2 cup oil
1 tablespoon each anise
  and fennel seeds
1 packet active yeast
  (10 grams)
1 teaspoon sugar
1 cup warm water
1/4 tablespoon salt
1 cup Warm water for
  kneading

Method

1. Sift flour and put it into a deep metal bowl. Make a well in the middle and add sesame seeds.

2. Heat ghee and oil to boiling. Pour over sesame seeds, stirring continuously until seeds turn golden in color. Mix ingredients well until ghee and oil are well absorbed.

3. Add anise and fennel seeds and mix.

4. Prepare yeast by adding sugar to it and then dissolving in 1 cup warm water. Add to flour. Knead well into flour using as much warm water as needed. Set aside 1 hour to rise.

5. Divide dough into pieces and flatten each with hands into 3 cm wide strips. Cut diagonally with a knife into small pieces and bake in a hot oven for 10 minutes until tops are lightly browned.

331

Jams

P reserving fruit by cooking it with sugar is an age-old practice in Egypt, and many varieties of fruit can be found all the year round. During the winter there are oranges, dates, and carrots available cheaply with which to make fresh and nutritious jams, but in the summer there is an even wider choice, including strawberries, apricots, peaches, plum, figs, or guavas. Keeping jams refrigerated means they can be preserved for up to six months.

Strawberry Jam

Ingredients
1 kilogram strawberries
1 kilogram sugar
Juice of 1 lime

Method

1. Wash strawberries well and remove stems. Add sugar, place over heat and stir.

2. Bring to a boil, removing any froth that forms, then lower heat and simmer until cooked (about 1 hour).

3. Add lime juice toward the end of cooking, about 5 minutes before strawberries are done. Remove from heat and cool.

4. Spoon into clean, dry jars, seal tightly, and store in refrigerator. They will safely keep there for up to 6 months.

Apricot Jam

Ingredients
1 kilogram pitted apricots
1 kilogram sugar
1/2 cup water
Juice of 1 lime

Method

1. Wash apricots. Weigh and add sugar (sugar must be equal to pitted apricot weight). Set aside for 2 hours.

2. Add water and place over heat, stirring until apricots come to a boil. Remove any froth that forms. Lower heat and simmer until fully cooked (about 1 hour).

3. Add lime juice 5 minutes before turning off heat. Remove from heat and cool.

4. Spoon into clean, dry jars, seal tightly. Store in refrigerator. They will safely keep there for up to 6 months.

Plum Jam

Ingredients
1 kilogram pitted plums
1 kilogram sugar
1/2 cup water
Juice of 1 lime

Method

Same as for Apricot Jam.

Fig Jam

Ingredients
1 kilogram figs
1 kilogram sugar
Juice of 1 lime
1/4 teaspoon ground cloves

Method

1. Wash, peel, and cube figs. Place in alternate layers with sugar and set aside for 6 hours.

2. Cook over low heat, stirring, until syrup thickens. Remove any froth that forms. Add lime juice and cloves. Set aside to cool.

3. Spoon into clean, dry jars, seal tightly, and store in refrigerator. The jam will safely keep there for up to 6 months.

Guava Jam

Ingredients

1 kilogram pureed guava

1 kilogram sugar

1/2 cup water

Juice of 1 lime

Method

1. Wash guavas and remove ends with a knife. Cut into pieces and blend in a blender. Strain.

2. Add sugar and water and stir well. Place over low heat, stirring. Remove any froth that forms.

3. Add lime juice 5 minutes before removing from heat. Set aside to cool.

4. Spoon into clean, dry jars, seal tightly, and store in refrigerator. The jam will safely keep there for up to 6 months.

Peach Jam

Ingredients

1 kilogram pitted peaches

1 kilogram sugar

1/2 cup water

Juice of 1 lime

Method

Same as for Apricot Jam.

Note: Most jams need about 1 hour to cook.

Carrot Jam

Ingredients

1 kilogram carrots

tangerine peel of 2 fruits

1 kilogram sugar

Juice of 1 lime

Method

1. Wash carrots, scrape skin, and grind them with tangerine peel.

2. Place ground carrot and sugar in alternate layers and set aside for 6 hours. Simmer over low heat, stirring from time to time. Remove any froth that forms.

3. When almost done, add lime juice and boil for an extra 5 minutes. Remove from heat and cool.

4. Spoon into clean, dry jars, seal tightly, and store in refrigerator. They will safely keep there for up to 6 months.

Yellow Date Jam
(Mirabat balah simani)

Ingredients

80 yellow dates

2 cups water

1/4 kilogram almonds,
  boiled and peeled,
  then halved

1 kilogram sugar

1 tablespoon ground
  cloves

Peel of two tangerines,
  washed and finely
  chopped

Juice of 1 lime

Method

1. Peel dates and place in a pot with water. Cook over heat for 10 minutes. Remove dates.

2. Use the thin end of a knife to push pits from the dates lengthwise. Replace with an almond half.

3. Add sugar to the water and bring to a boil. Add dates, cloves, and tangerine peel and simmer until syrup thickens. Add lime juice 5 minutes before turning off heat. Cool.

4. Spoon into clean, dry jars, seal tightly, and store in refrigerator. They will safely keep there for up to 6 months.

Apple Jam

Ingredients
1 kilogram washed, peeled and cored apples
1 cup water
Juice of 2 limes
1 kilogram sugar

Method

1. Cut apples into slices and place in water to which the juice of 1 lime has been added.

2. Boil for 10 minutes, then drain.

3. Add sugar to apple water and bring to a boil, stirring to dissolve. Add apples and simmer until apples are done, about 1 hour. Remove any froth that forms.

4. Add the juice of 1 lime to the jam and boil for another 5 minutes. Cool.

5. Spoon into clean, dry jars, seal tightly, and store in refrigerator. The jam will safely keep there for up to 6 months.

Pear Jam

Ingredients
1 kilogram washed, peeled and cored firm pears
1 cup water
Juice of 1 lime
1 kilogram sugar

Method

Same as for Apple Jam.

Beverages

S ince ancient times, Egyptians have used their own particular ingredients for special drinks, either to warm the body in winter, such as cinna- mon, ginger, *sahlab* (orchid drink), or chickpea drink, or to keep the body cool with carob, doum palm, hibiscus, liquorice, or dried tamarind.

Spiced Fenugreek *(Hilba mihawiga)*

Ingredients

2 tablespoons sesame
  seeds
2 tablespoons ghee
1/8 kilogram ready-spiced
  fenugreek *(Hilba
  Mihawiga)*
1/2 liter water
4 tablespoons sugar
1 tablespoon toasted
  chopped hazelnuts
  per cup

Method

1. Fry sesame seeds in ghee until golden. Add fenugreek and stir. Add water and sugar and continue stirring.

2. Cook over heat until mixture thickens. Pour into cups and spoon ground hazelnuts on top. Serve hot.

Fried Mughat (Mughat mihamar)

Ingredients

2 tablespoons sesame
   seeds
2 tablespoons ghee
1/8 kilogram glossoste-
   mum bruguiere
   (mughat)
1/2 liter water
4 tablespoons sugar
1 tablespoon toasted
   chopped hazelnuts
   per cup

Method

1. Fry sesame seeds in ghee until golden. Add fenugreek and stir. Add water and sugar and continue stirring.

2. Cook over heat until mixture thickens. Pour into cups and spoon ground hazelnuts on top. Serve hot.

Carob Drink
(Kharub)

Ingredients
1 cup sugar
1 cup ground carob
1 liter water

Method

1. Place sugar over medium heat, stirring until it becomes caramel colored. Add carob and stir for a little while.

2. Add water and boil for 5 minutes. Remove from heat.

3. Set aside to soak for 6 hours, then strain and pour into clean glass bottles. Refrigerate for 2 to 3 days.

Dum Palm Drink

Ingredients
1 cup sugar
1 cup ground dum
1 liter water

Method

Same steps as for Carob Drink

Dried Tamarind

Ingredients

1/4 kilogram dried
   tamarind
1 1/2 liter water
2 cups sugar

Method

1. Wash tamarind, cover
   with water, and boil for
   5 minutes. Set aside
   to soak for 6 hours.

2. Drain first through a
   cheesecloth-lined
   sieve, then through a
   paper-towel lined sieve
   until a clear, colored
   liquid is achieved.

3. Sweeten with sugar,
   bottle, and refrigerate.

Liquorice Drink *('Irq sus)*

Ingredients

1/8 kilogram liquorice
   powder
1 tablespoon baking
   soda
1 1/2 liters water

Method

1. Rub liquorice well
   with baking soda and
   sprinkle with a little
   water. Set aside in
   direct sunlight if
   possible for 30 minutes
   until color turns black.

2. Dissolve in water and
   set aside to soak for 30
   minutes. Strain through
   a cheesecloth-lined
   sieve, then refrigerate.

3. To serve, pour into
   glasses from high
   above so that the aera-
   tion forms bubbles.

Hibiscus
(Karkadih)

Ingredients
1/8 kilogram dried karkadah
1 liter water
1/2 cup sugar

Method

1. Rinse karkadah and cover with water. Place over heat for 5 minutes until it boils.

2. Set aside to soak for at least 1 hour. Strain and sweeten.

3. Refrigerate and serve cold.

Dates in Milk

Ingredients
1/4 kilogram dried dates
1/2 liter milk

Method

1. Wash dates, cut them in half, and remove pits.

2. Boil milk and add dates. Simmer for 15 minutes in a covered saucepan.

3. Set aside to soak for 2 hours. Serve warm.

Pressed Apricot Drink
(Qamar al-din)

Ingredients
1/2 kilogram pressed apricot sheets
1/2 cup sugar
1 liter water

Method

1. Cut pressed apricot sheet into small pieces. Add sugar and water and boil for 5 minutes. Set aside to soak for at least 1 hour.

2. Sieve and store in refrigerator. Drink cold.

Whole Grain Wheat in Milk (Bilila bi-l-laban)

Ingredients
1 cup whole wheat grains
1 liter water
1/2 liter milk
1 cup sugar
Grated coconut

Method

1. Wash wheat and cover with water. Cook for 10 minutes, then set aside to soak for 8 hours. Bring to a boil, then lower heat to a simmer for 2 hours.

2. Add milk, sweeten with sugar, and serve hot with grated coconut spooned on the top.

Cinnamon and Ginger Drink

Ingredients
1 tablespoon cinnamon
1/4 teaspoon ginger
1 tablespoon sugar
1 cup water
Toasted, ground hazelnuts

Method

Dissolve cinnamon, ginger, and sugar in water and bring to a boil. Pour into a large teacup and spoon nuts on the top. Serve hot.

Milk with Cinnamon

Ingredients
1 tablespoon cinnamon
1 tablespoon sugar
1 cup milk
Ground toasted hazelnuts

Method

Dissolve cinnamon and sugar in milk. Bring to a boil, then pour into a large teacup and spoon ground nuts on the top. Serve hot.

Boiled Fenugreek

Ingredients
1/4 kilogram fenugreek seeds
1 liter water
3 tablespoons sugar
Milk, optional

Method

1. Clean and wash fenugreek seeds. Cover with water and place over heat for 15 minutes. Remove from heat and set aside to soak for 1 hour.

2. Sweeten with sugar and serve. May add milk if desired.

Coconut Drink
(Subia)

Ingredients
1 cup grated coconut
1 liter milk
1/4 kilogram sugar
1 tablespoon vanilla
1/2 cup rice starch

Method

Soak coconut in milk for 1 hour. Add sugar, vanilla, and rice starch and blend in blender. Serve cold.

Note: Rice starch can be replaced with rice water, made with 1/2 cup rice boiled in two liters of water for 10 minutes. Strain and use water. Subia must be refrigerated and used within 24 hours.

Orchid Drink *(Sahlab)*

Ingredients
2 tablespoons *sahlab*
2 tablespoons sugar
1 cup milk
Chopped hazelnuts
Grated coconut

Method

1. Dissolve *sahlab* and sugar in milk. Cook over medium heat, stirring until mixture thickens.

2. Pour into a teacup, garnish with nuts and coconut and serve hot.

Chickpea Drink *(Halbasa)*

Ingredients
1/4 kilogram chickpeas
1 liter water
1/2 tablespoon salt
1/4 teaspoon red pepper
1/4 teaspoon cumin
Juice of 1 lime

Method

1. Soak chickpeas in water for 12 hours. Change water then boil for 4 hours.

2. Add salt, red pepper, cumin, and lime juice. Serve hot.

Assorted Recipes

Pastrami *(Bastirma)*

Ingredients

Ingredients
1 beef roast (fillet)
1 cup coarse-grained salt
1 head garlic, crushed
1/8 kilogram ground fenugreek
1/8 kilogram sweet (mild) paprika
Water

Method

1. Rinse beef roast and dry well using paper towels. Cover completely with salt on all sides.

2. Wrap in a piece of clean cloth and set aside for 12 hours, placing a heavy weight on top of the meat to help drain excess liquid. Refrigerate for food safety.

3. Prepare crust for *bastirma* by combining garlic, fenugreek, sweet paprika, and enough water to form a thick paste.

4. Clean meat with a piece of cloth. Make a hole at one end of the beef and tie a piece of string through the hole.

5. Coat well with the garlic and fenugreek paste, covering on all sides. Wet hands and smooth over meat to even out paste and completely seal.

6. Hang in a place exposed to fresh air for at least 2 weeks before use.

Local Sausages *(Suguq)*

Ingredients

Ingredients
1 kilogram ground lean beef
Salt, pepper, and mixed spices (peppercorns, nutmeg, cumin, cinnamon, cloves, bay leaves)
1/8 kilogram pine nuts
Pieces of sheep tail fat
Small salted sheep intestines (obtained from a butcher)

Method

1. Mix beef, salt, pepper, spices, pine nuts, and fat well with hands until thoroughly blended.

2. Soak salted intestines in water for 1 hour, then rinse under running water to wash off salt.

3. Stuff intestines with beef mixture to form suguq by using the special machine for this purpose. Hang for a while to dry, then store in a freezer until use.

Salted Mullet (Fisikh)

Ingredients

1/2 kilogram medium
   grain salt
1 tablespoon red pepper
1 kilogram gray mullet fish

To serve:
Corn oil
2 tablespoons lime juice
2 sweet peppers, chopped
Green onions, chopped

Method

1. Use a piece of cloth to rub fish dry. Mix salt and red pepper. Stuff fish gills with salt and red pepper mix and place on absorbent paper in direct sunlight for 24 hours to get rid of excess water.

2. Prepare a wooden box by lining the bottom with a thick layer of salt, then arrange alternate layers of fish and salt.

3. Close box tightly and place in a dark place for 21 days to a month. Make sure that a container is placed under the box to hold the excess liquid that drains out.

4. Remove fish from salt. Wash right before serving and cut each into two halves. Serve with oil, lime juice, chopped sweet pepper, and green onions.

Salted Sardines

Ingredients

1 kilogram sardines
1/2 kilogram coarse salt
1 tablespoon red pepper

Method

1. Dry sardines using a clean piece of cloth. Set in the sun to dry for 24 hours.

2. Place a little salt and red pepper in the bottom of a large plastic bag. Arrange sardines and salt and pepper mixture in alternate layers, making sure that the last layer is salt and pepper.

3. Press air out of the bag, close tightly and store in a dark place for 15 days before using.

Dried Green Mallow
(*Mulukhiyya*)

Ingredients
2 kilograms green mallow

Method

1. Wash and dry green mallow leaves. Place on a clean piece of cloth in direct sunlight for 5 to 7 days until leaves are completely dried.

2. Rub dried leaves between the palms of the hands, then press leaves through a coarse sieve or sifter. Store in plastic bags in a dry cool place or in a refrigerator. Dried mulukhiyya should be used as a powder and placed immediately in broth.

Dried Caviar

Ingredients
caviar

Method

Wash caviar fingers and dry with absorbent paper. Cover with a thick layer of salt and place in direct sunlight for 3 days until completely dry.

Dried Okra

Ingredients
1 kilogram green okra
A large needle and thread

Method

1. Wash okra and dry with a towel. Using the needle and a long piece of thread, thread okra through the cap ends into long chains.

2. Hang to dry in direct sunlight for about 15 days, until okra is completely dried and yellowish in color. Store in a dry place until use. Okra must be soaked in water for 2 hours before cooking.

Dried Peas

Ingredients
1 kilogram green peas

Method

1. Shell peas and wash. Expose to direct sunlight for 10 days to 2 weeks until completely dried, like grains.

2. Store in plastic bags in a dry place until use. Peas must be soaked for about 2 hours in water before cooking.

Lupines

Ingredients
1/2 kilogram lupines
Lime juice
Cumin
Red pepper

Method

1. Boil lupines for 1 hour, then soak in water for 5 days, changing the water every 12 hours.

2. Sprinkle lupines with salt on the fifth day, then store in the refrigerator. Add lime juice, cumin, and a little red pepper directly before serving.

349

Green Fenugreek

Ingredients
1/2 kilogram fenugreek

Method

1. Soak fenugreek in water for 12 hours, then drain in a colander.

2. Cover with a piece of wet, thin cloth and set aside for 5 days. Make sure that the cloth is always kept wet by frequently sprinkling it with water. The fenugreek is ready when long stems are sprouted. Store in a refrigerator until use.

Sprouted Baked Broad Beans
(Ful miqili)

Ingredients
1/2 kilogram broad beans
Salt
Cumin
Red pepper
Lime juice
1 cup water

Method

1. Wash broad beans. Soak in water for 12 hours, then place in a colander and cover with a piece of wet, thin cloth for 2 days until white ends sprout. Make sure that the cloth is always kept wet by frequently sprinkling it with water.

2. Place beans in an oven of medium heat for 30 minutes, then remove. Sprinkle with salt, cumin, red pepper, lime juice, and water. Store in the refrigerator.

Note: Chickpeas can be prepared following the same technique.

Daily Meals

The nutritional values of individual foods must be considered when planning daily meals so as to meet all the body's requirements. Foods are divided into 3 basic groups:

Foods that Build

Meats, fish, eggs, cheese, milk, and milk products, legumes (such as beans, lentils, chickpeas, and nuts).

Foods that Protect

Vegetables, such as spinach, cabbage, okra, radishes, lettuce, tomatoes.
Fruits, such as oranges, grapes, dates, bananas, figs, pears.

Foods that Give Energy

Grains, bread, pasta, rice, potatoes, honey, sugar, fats.

To form a balanced meal, one or more foods from each group must be selected. Make sure that each meal contains enough foods that build. The more expensive protein foods can be replaced with cheaper kinds such as cottage cheese and other milk products as well as different kinds of legumes.

Each meal should contain one or more foods that protect. Vitamin C is lost by cooking, so the menu must include fresh salads and fruits.

Each meal should contain some foods that give energy such as rice, bread or pasta, as well as the fats and oils that are part of the cooking process.

To ensure that the body gets its requirement of the different nutrients, a wide variety of foods must be consumed. Menus should vary from one meal to the other.

Breakfast Menus

- Stewed broad beans with oil and lime juice, *baladi* (local) bread, white cheese, tomatoes, tea with milk.
- Boiled eggs, *duqqa* with thyme, baladi bread, molasses with tahini, tea with milk.
- Fried, crushed bean patties, *baladi* bread, jam and butter, tea with milk.
- Vermicelli with sugar and milk, *rumi* cheese, *baladi* bread, tea with milk.

Lunch Menus

- Stewed spinach with chickpeas, rice with tomatoes, green salad or pickled limes, bananas and oranges.
- Shank soup, shank *fatta* with garlic and vinegar, yogurt salad, tripe with chickpeas, seasonal fruit.
- Vegetables and bone soup, mixed stuffed dolma, meat with cumin, yogurt salad, orange and carrot pudding.
- Green mallow (*mulukhiyya*) with rabbit, rabbit soup with rosamarina pasta, green salad, *baklava* with nuts.
- Brown lentils with rice and pasta, boiled and fried eggs, eggplant salad with vinegar and fresh garlic, beetroot salad, pudding with nuts.
- Grilled fish, white rice cooked in oil, local salad, eggplant and tahini salad, baklava with nuts.

Dinner Menus

In most cases, foods eaten at dinner are similar to those eaten at breakfast, with the optional addition of such foods as liver and fried *suguq*.

Menus for Feasts and Special Occasions

In Egypt, people are accustomed to celebrating special occasions by preparing special foods and feasting for these special occasions, traditions for which the Egyptians are well-known.

The Month of Ramadan

The *iftar* meal (eaten at sunset when the daily fast is broken) must consist of easily digested foods that are sufficient to last until the *suhur* meal (eaten just before dawn, the last meal before the daily fast begins). It is important to start *iftar* with a bowl of hot soup to stimulate the digestive tract after a long period of fasting. The meal must also include salad, to provide the body with vitamins and minerals. Dessert is also essential as a source of energy.

Samples of Iftar Menus for the Month of Ramadan

• Dates in milk, chicken broth, fried chicken, green mallow (*mulukhiyya*), local bread or rice, mixed pickles, *qata'if* with nuts.

• Pressed apricot drink, tomato soup, okra casserole, rice, green salad, *kunafa* with pudding.

• Fruit compote, lentil soup, pot Kebabs, pasta with béchamel sauce, beetroot salad, apricot pudding.

• Carob drink, fish soup, fish and potato casserole, fisherman's-style rice, eggplant salad with tomatoes, vinegar and garlic, *baklava* with nuts.

• Dried tamarind drink, strained vegetable soup, baked leg of lamb, *khalta* rice, green salad, *qata'if* with pudding.

• Dates in milk, vegetable soup, pan of stewed broad beans with tomatoes and eggs, eggplant stuffed with garlic and green pepper, *Umm 'Ali*.

• Pressed apricot drink, fisherman's-style fish soup, seafood rice, fried red mullet or sole, local salad, tahini salad, assabi zaynab.

The Suhur Meal

Milk and milk products such as cheese and yogurt must be served along with fruits, legumes such as broad beans and lentil soup, as well as bread.

'Id al-Fitr
(The feast following Ramadan)

At this feast, people are accustomed to eating fish, particularly salted cod, besides a wide assortment of biscuits including *ka'k*, *ghurayiba*, biscuits with pitted dates, biscuits with anise seeds and petit four biscuits.

'Id al-Adha (Bairam Feast)

At this feast, people are accustomed to eating lamb meat, prepared in all different ways and forms: as broth, baked leg of lamb, *fatta*, grilled kidney and liver, fried or with cumin, and a pan of *ruqaq*. They eat lupines and fruits after the meat to help digestion.

Other Islamic Religious Occasions

Islamic New Year (The first day of the Islamic month of Muharam). People eat meat-stuffed dough, poultry such as ducks and geese, fried chicken, and *khalta* rice. Seasonal sweets are also served (made from sesame, chickpeas, and peanuts, as well as turkish delight and *kishk*)

'Ashura Season *(Musim 'Ashura)* (The 10th of the Islamic month of Muharam). Like other "seasons," people serve poultry or meat and mixed vegetables such as green mallow (*mulukhiyya*), okra or peas. The dessert, *'ashura*, is an essential dish on this occasion. It is served along with couscous and seasonal sweets.

The birth of the Prophet (The eve of the 12th of the Islamic month of *Rabi' al-Awal*. Poultry, meats, and seasonal sweets are usually served.

Ragab Season (The eve of the 27th of the Islamic month of Ragab). This celebrates *"al-isra' wa almi'rag."* Poultry, meats, vegetables, and seasonal sweets are usually served.

Mid Sha'ban (the eve of the 15th of the Islamic month of Sha'ban). This celebrates the change of the Islamic direction of prayer from al-Aqsa Mosque to the ka'ba in Mecca. Poultry, meats, cooked vegetables, and seasonal sweets are served.

Samples of Dinner Party Menus

A Meat Feast:
- Meat broth
- Oven baked leg of lamb or back of lamb with rice
- Pan of *ruqaq* with ground meat
- Okra and lamb casserole
- Stuffed grape leaves and zucchini with ground meat

- Eggplant with béchamel sauce and white rice
- Green salad, beetroot salad, mixed pickles
- A tray of *kunafa* or *baklava* with nuts
- Poor man's *kishk* and seasonal fruits

A Poultry Feast:
- Poultry broth (according to the bird cooked)
- Fried duck or local chicken or pigeons stuffed with cracked wheat (more than one kind of bird may be served).
- Khalta rice, green mallow (*mulukhiyya*), burani okra
- Chicken *kishk*, *ruqaq* with ground meat, mixed pickles
- Potato salad, green salad
- Prunes with cream, *balah al-sham*, seasonal fruits

A Seafood Feast:
Fish broth
- Boiled large shrimp, oyster or mussel casserole
- Seafood rice, fried fish fillet
- Sibia casserole, local salad, eggplant and tahini salad with vinegar and garlic
- Apricot pudding, *basima*, seasonal fruits

Coptic Christian Fasting

Copts fast on and around numerous holidays, and on regular days of the week, adding up to more than half the days in the year. Those who keep the fast refrain from eating anything that comes from a living creature with a soul (for example, meat, chicken, eggs, milk, cheese, butter, and ghee). These fasts are as follows:

- **The Christmas (or 'short') Fast**, which lasts for forty-three days. It begins in the last week of November and continues until January 7. Those fasting are permitted to eat fish, except on Wednesdays and Fridays. The fast during these days is intermittent, from 12 midnight to 12 noon the next day, and is not compulsory.
- **The Easter (or 'long') Fast**, which lasts for fifty-five days when the eating of fish is not permitted.
- **The Virgin's Fast**, fourteen days from August 7 to August 21.
- **The Apostles' Fast**, which begins fifty days after Easter. This can last anywhere between two weeks and thirty days depending on the church.
- **Fasting Wednesdays and Fridays** of each week.

Coptic Festivals and Holidays

1. The New Year is celebrated on December 31. The main course served on the occasion is fish and shrimps, since this celebration is during the fasting period.

2. Christmas celebrations for Copts (Eastern Christians) are on January 7 (Western Christians celebrate on December 25).

The main course is eaten in the evening after Mass. It usually consists of:

- Boiled meat
- Fried hardboiled eggs
- Pureed potatoes
- Macaroni with béchamel sauce

The main course of Sunday lunch is eaten the next day at lunch and consists of:

- Duck stuffed with hulled wheat (cooked

green wheat), onions, and giblets (the liver and gizzards of the bird)
• Turkey stuffed with onions and liver, roasted and basted with orange juice
• Vegetables such as *mulukhiyya* and okra
• Different varieties of cakes and biscuits

3. On Epiphany (19 January), the following foods are served:
• Colocasia cooked with other vegetables, with meat or poultry, and stewed and fried colocasia
• Rice baked in the oven with milk, and with giblets
• Sugarcane, oranges, and tangerines

4. Coptic Easter sometimes coincides with Western Easter and sometimes it can be up to five weeks after it.

5. On Jacob's Wednesday, hulled wheat (cooked green wheat) with tomatoes is served.

6. On Holy Thursday, cooked brown lentils are eaten.

7. On Good Friday, bean sprouts *(ful nabit)*, bean cakes (*ta'miya*), and pressed apricot pudding (*'amar al-din*) are eaten.

8. On Holy Saturday, leftovers from the previous day, Good Friday, are eaten.

9. On Easter Sunday, the same dishes eaten during Christmas are served.

Shamm al-Nisim

On this spring holiday (which coincides with the second day of Coptic Easter), people are accustomed to eating salted mullet (*fisikh*), green onions, lettuce, green chickpeas, colored eggs, lupines, green fenugreek, and sprouted baked broad beans.

Index